CRIB QUILTS
AND
OTHER SMALL WONDERS

1. Pot of Flowers appliqué. c. 1860. 44½″ x 35″. This exhilarating example of naïve design shows a delight in strong color and handsome quilting. Historic Deerfield, Inc., Deerfield, Massachusetts.

CRIB QUILTS
and Other Small Wonders

Including complete patterns and instructions
for making your own crib quilts

Thos. K. Woodard

Blanche Greenstein

BONANZA BOOKS
NEW YORK

Quilts for which no owner has been listed, as well as a number of those designated *private collection*, are from the authors' collection or have been supplied by Thos. K. Woodard: American Antiques & Quilts, N.Y.C.

Names and locations of the makers of the quilts have been included when such information was available to the authors.

This 1988 edition is published by Bonanza Books, distributed by Crown Publishers, Inc., 225 Park Avenue South, New York, New York 10003, by arrangement with E.P. Dutton.

Manufactured in Hong Kong

Library of Congress Cataloging-in-Publication Data

Woodard, Thomas K.
  [Crib quilts and other small wonders]
  Reprint. Originally published: Crib quilts and other small wonders. 1st ed. New York : Dutton, 1981.
  1. Crib quilts—United States.   2. Crib quilts—Patterns.
I. Greenstein, Blanche.   II. Title.
NK9112.W67   1988
746.9′7—dc19   87-32658
ISBN 0-517-65871-2

h g f e d c b a

To our families and friends

ACKNOWLEDGMENTS

Walter Bachner; Caroline Baker; Baltimore Museum of Art, Baltimore, Maryland; Darwin Bearley; Linda and Irwin Berman; Barbara Bersell; Dr. and Mrs. Ronald Brady; Mr. and Mrs. Peter M. Brant; Karey Patterson Bresenhan; Sally Clark; Barry Cohen; Solomon Cohen; Judy Corman; Suzanne Courcier; Nancy Crow; Paul and Muffin Cunnion; Lindsay Lee Davison; Marcia Delman; Christophe de Menil; Tony Ellis; Kathy and Fred Epstein; Molly Epstein; Esprit de Corps, San Francisco; Patricia Etheridge; Georgia Feasal; Helaine and Burton Fendelman; Mr. and Mrs. Peter Findlay; M. Finkel and Daughter; Raymond and Nancy Fisher; Pie Galinat; Bill Gallick; Mr. and Mrs. Ivan Gerson; Cora Ginsburg; Hovey and Evelyn Gleason; Greenfield Village and Henry Ford Museum, Dearborn, Michigan; André Gürtler; Rebecca Haarer; Phyllis Haders; Dr. and Mrs. Donald Herr; Timothy and Pamela Hill; Historic Deerfield, Inc., Deerfield, Massachusetts; Jonathan Holstein; Glendora Hutson; Jay Johnson: America's Folk Heritage Gallery; Lena Kaplan; Dena S. Katzenberg; Kelter-Malcé Antiques; Hazel B. Kile; Robert E. Kinnaman and Brian A. Ramaekers; Kiracofe and Kile; Phyllis Kirkpatrick; Mr. and Mrs. Ronald Lauder; Donald Leiby; The Library of Congress, Washington, D.C.; Iona Lincoln; Gloria List; Richard and Rosemarie Machmer; Mr. and Mrs. Foster McCarl, Jr.; Frank and Karen Miehle; Myron Miller; Sandra Mitchell; John C. Newcomer; Jane Nylander; Old Sturbridge Village, Sturbridge, Massachusetts; Patsy Orlofsky, Textile Conservation Center; Louise Perrin; Joy and Jack Piscopo; Plain Sewing, Fay Walters; David Pottinger; Marilyn Rey; Stella Rubin; Mr. and Mrs. Sherman Saperstein; Raymond Saroff; George E. Schoellkopf Gallery; Kathy and John Schoemer; Stephen and Eleanor Score; Robert Self; Jacqueline and John Sideli; Mr. and Mrs. Richard Flanders Smith; Grace and Elliot Snyder; Nancy and Gary Stass; Betty Sterling; Jayme Stewart; Susan Burrows Swan; H. John and Joan L. Thayer; Gail van der Hoof; Arthur Vitols, Helga Photo Studio; Alice Baldridge Wainwright; Hilda Waters; Elizabeth Weisman; Mike Wigg; Robert Wilkins; The Henry Francis du Pont Winterthur Museum, Winterthur, Delaware; Deborah Wiss; Mr. and Mrs. Eugene Zuriff.

For his invaluable assistance, a special thank you to our editor, Cyril I. Nelson, whose superior standards have been a continuing source of encouragement and inspiration.

CONTENTS

INTRODUCTION

The history of textiles and of the development of quilting in America have been explored in both general and specialized volumes by many authors. These and other valuable sources of information are listed in the Bibliography and contain a wealth of specific, if sometimes contradictory, information.

With the recent surge of interest in collecting American folk art, there has developed an unprecedented fascination with crib quilts among collectors. In fact, fine crib quilts and Amish quilts (both of which were taken for granted for years but are now somewhat scarce) are two of the most sought-after items in the entire antiques market. Inevitably, with this sudden, in some cases fanatic, enthusiasm for crib quilts, we have seen prices soar. Because crib quilts are small, they can be hung as "textile paintings" in spaces that cannot accommodate full-size quilts. And viewed as original works of art, they still are a bargain, even at the dramatically increased prices recently recorded. One crib quilt that we sold in our gallery three years ago for under $100 is now appraised at $600. Another, purchased originally for $300 in 1976, is now worth over $4,000.

Of course, not all crib quilts are rising in value as quickly. Few are so desirable, and some are not even crib quilts at all, but rather cutdown versions of full-size quilts or reproductions of crib quilts. These, which are glutting the market and are even sold at the most famous auction houses, are worth no more than any other newly made craft item. Some of the most convincing fakes have been sold as old Amish crib and doll quilts and are very skillfully stitched miniatures of the traditional Diamond and Bar patterns (the Sunshine and Shadow design is, presumably, too complex and time-consuming to reproduce), using beautiful old Amish materials in characteristic colors. Most authentic old Amish crib and doll quilts were quite primitive—sometimes just random patches, made by children for fun or practice.

So that we might better understand this preoccupation with small quilts and related textiles, we set out to explore this phenomenon, to look into the crib quilt's part in America's past, its place in American life from the early days to the present. Most important, the many full-color illustrations in this book faithfully reproduce the unique qualities of color, form, and design achieved by anonymous American folk artists.

Of special interest to us were the makers' feelings, the sentiments—rather than the sentimentality—of people who chose to make beautiful crib quilts, often under difficult physical and emotional circumstances. We were curious about the motives impelling these artists and hoped that we could increase our understanding of their desires, the folk art through which they expressed themselves, and possibly even something about their descendants—ourselves.

DEFINITIONS AND GENERAL HISTORY

The story of crib quilts in early America must be largely inferred from records of household inventories, probate records, and diaries, which fortunately have been preserved by libraries, museums, and historical societies. Some are in manuscript form, several have been transferred to microfilm for a more permanent record, and a few have been published and are readily available in bookstores (see Bibliography). In any form, these records are important and fascinating treasures of information about what life was like in the first years of America.

It is impossible to say who made the first crib quilt, or to whom the idea first occurred to make a small quilted spread of pieced or appliqué work complete within itself and never intended to be any size but small.

The idea of quilting ties us to ancient history, when it was discovered that two layers of material filled with some light stuffing material provided excellent protection and insulation against both heat and cold.

The word *quilt* derives from the Latin word *culcita*, meaning a stuffed sack, mattress, or cushion. It comes into English from the Old French word *coilte* or *cuilte*. Today, the word *quilt* refers to two cloths sewn together with a soft filling between the two layers. Although it usually means a kind of "textile sandwich," the general term also includes some exceptions, such as the single layered, all-white candlewick spread illustrated in figure 2 ("Little Sadie Maud") and the Log Cabin, figure 50, which is layered but has no filling.

A crib quilt, then, is simply a small textile sandwich. The average size of a *crib* or *cradle* quilt—the terms are used interchangeably here—is one square yard, although many were made smaller or larger, or in varying proportions of length and width. The predominance of one square yard as the size chosen for crib quilts recalls a tradition in seventeenth- and eighteenth-century England of a white handkerchief

2. "Little Sadie Maud" summer spread. Second half of nineteenth century. 48″ x 33″. "White work" has been popular for centuries in many forms, and this entertaining miniature is a rare example of candlewick embroidery done for a child. Private collection.

offering by a woman to her country parish. A reference to this custom can be found in the register book of Wickenby, Lincolnshire, dating from the early seventeenth century: "The chrysom and a grace penny is always to be given at ye woman's churching. The chrysom must be a yard of fine Lennen Long and a full yard in width." [1] The white handkerchief evidently represented the *chrisom* cloth, a special cloth in which the baby was wrapped for the christening in earlier times.

Doll quilts are often less than twelve inches long, and trundle bed or cot quilts sometimes reach over five feet in length. Often one discovers a small-size quilt, which was originally full size, but has been cut down to fit a smaller bed or to salvage a worn spread in the frugal tradition of the American homemaker. Although such "cutdowns" are interesting examples of

the sensible recycling of very scarce materials in the early days of this country, they are not crib quilts in the strict sense of the term. We also, obviously, must eliminate modern cutdowns, quilts that have recently been made smaller to benefit from the intense competition in collecting crib quilts.

Although the term *crib quilt* implies that it was intended for use by infants, the majority of those illustrated in these pages have survived in fine condition, and some show no signs of use. This indicates that perhaps the most beautiful and interesting crib quilts were made more as a creative expression, enhanced beyond the purely functional, and treasured as such by the owner. While it is true that numerous crib covers were made primarily for utilitarian purposes, examples of this type, such as tied or tufted comforters made from work clothes or other coarser materials, lack the design and individuality of our most interesting folk art, and are often very badly worn from the rugged use for which they were intended.

Crib quilts trace their history to ancient times. From the period of the Egyptian First Dynasty (c. 3000 B.C.) people have known the advantages of quilting. An ivory carving of a pharaoh from that period, now at The British Museum, wears the earliest known quilted garment.

Probably the oldest existing quilt dates from around 100 B.C. and is in the form of a carpet discovered in Mongolia in the tomb of an ancient Siberian chieftain. During the Middle Ages and the Renaissance quilting appeared in the form of defensive armor, wall hangings, curtains, bedcovers, and quilted undergarments. The armor consisted of an outer layer of linen or leather padded with wool, cotton, or flax.

Were it not for the present resurgence of interest in quilting, the story of one of the most refined and popular forms of American folk art might have ended with the last great quilting revival in the 1920s and 1930s. A century ago quilting was at its height; frugal housewives, using bits and scraps of cloth, transcended their mundane existence to become astonishing folk artists. With intuitive sense of design these inventive women created decorative objects for the home that may never by matched in originality, vigor, charm, and beauty. The characteristics of these artistic expressions closely reflect the way of life from which they sprang, conditions that no longer exist in modern times. The high standards of quilting established in the nineteenth century provide both constant inspiration and an awesome challenge to today's quilters.

THE HISTORY OF INFANT CLOTHING

To begin, let us take a look at certain social and cultural mores of ancient history that, although they now

3. Peony variation. 1979. Berkeley, California. 44″ x 36″. Made by Glendora Hutson. Inspired by the nineteenth-century Cactus Rose pattern, this contemporary variation captures the orderly, uncluttered vitality of another era's designs, and recalls for us past generations of extraordinary women artists. Collection of the artist.

seem remote, have left traces of their influence on the development of crib quilts.

Claudius Galen (c. A.D. 130–200), the court physician to Emperor Marcus Aurelius in Rome, was second only to Hippocrates in medical renown. A prolific writer, he produced more than 100 treatises dealing with various subjects, including the care and feeding of infants. As did his predecessors and his successors for many years thereafter, he subscribed to the theory that newborn infants must be bound or wrapped up tightly in swaddling clothes. These bands of cloth were widely regarded as a healthy and necessary means to give the correct shape to the body and limbs through pressure.[2]

An Italian physician, Paolo Bagellardo, was still recommending swaddling in the fifteenth century. He instructed the midwife to wrap "a linen cloth, not hard," around the newborn infant. He also gave detailed instructions on how to use the "bearing cloth," with notes on binding up the trunk and limbs; the main purpose was to give the child a proper shape.[3]

François Mauriceau published *Traité des maladies des femmes grosses* in Paris in 1668, a work that was translated into English and published in London five years later. Mauriceau was no different from his contemporaries in his support of the ancient fallacy that infants would not grow straight unless they were molded by tight binding:

. . . let his Arms and Legs be wrapped in his bed and stretched strait and swathed to keep them so, vis. his Arms along his sides and his Legs equally both together with a little of the bed between them that so they may not be galled by rubbing one another: after all this the Head must be kept steady and strait with a stay fastned on each side the Blancket, and then wrap the Child up in Mantles or Blanckets to keep it warm. He must be thus swaddled to give his little body a strait Figure, which is most decent and convenient for a Man and to accustom him to keep upon the Feet, for else he would go upon all four as most other Animals do.[4]

Swaddling disappeared gradually in the eighteenth century. In 1768 an anonymous essay "by a physician" was published by the Committee of the Foundling Hospital in London urging the abandonment of several age-old customs and introducing more progressive, rational methods. Titled "An Essay upon Nursing and the Management of Children from Their Birth to Three Years of Age," the work, which was credited to "William Cadogan, of Bristol, M.D." in subsequent editions, was a force in advancing new thought and had a strong influence in improving child care. In order to strengthen his case for change, he suggested to doubters that they "look over the Bills of Mortality, there he may observe that almost half the Number of those that fill up that black List are under five Years of Age." With that grave introduction, he proceeded:

The first great Mistake is that they (the ignorant) think a new-born Infant cannot be kept too warm: from this Prejudice they load it and bind it with Flannels, Wrappers, Swathes, Stays etc commonly called Cloaths, which all together are almost equal to its own Weight [he advises light loose garments, which he thinks] . . . would be sufficient for the Day, laying aside all those swathes, bandages, stays and contrivances, that are most ridiculously used to close and keep the Head in its Place and support the Body, as if Nature, exact Nature, had produced her chief Work, a human Creature, so carelessly unfinished as to want those idle Aids to make it perfect . . .[5]

At this same time an almanac was published with advice on the "easy rearing of children" by an anonymous writer,[6] who recommended that children sleep on top of quilts rather than feathers. This recommendation came approximately 100 years after John Locke had adequately covered the subject in *Some Thoughts Concerning Education* (1693):

Let his Bed be hard, and rather Quilts than

Feathers. Hard lodging strengthens the Parts, whereas being buryed every Night in Feathers melts and dissolves the Body . . . Besides, he that is used to hard lodgings at Home will not miss his Sleep (where he has most Need of it) in his travels abroad for want of his soft Bed, and his Pillows laid in Order.[7]

The New Theory of Generation by John Cooke, M.D., was published in London in 1762. According to the author, it was at least partly a compilation of other works, and, therefore, represents a cross section of current thought on infant management. In one of his chapters on newborn babies he advises:

If swathed up undo it directly to give room. But if they were not swathed but allowed as much freedom as puppies it would be much better for them as I have shewn in a former discourse on the cause of the surprising mortality of Infants under two years of age in the London Magazine for 1768 . . .[8]

This long-overdue warning against excessive swaddling was the beginning of the end of an obsolete custom.

The fifth edition of a book by George Armstrong, M.D., originally titled "An Essay on the Diseases Most Fatal to Infants to Which Are Added Rules to Be Observed in the Nursing of Children: with a Particular View to Those Who Are Brought up by Hand," appeared in London in 1808. First published in 1769, this edition contained an "Introduction by the Editor," which was significant because in it the reader is told that by now people have mostly given up the custom of "squeezing the baby into shape by tight swaddling." The editor also makes mention of his contemporaries having memories of the swaddling tradition within their lifetimes.[9]

By the second quarter of the nineteenth century, popular periodicals such as *The Family Magazine* carried articles recommending more freedom for a child's body in order to improve his physical state, and, of great importance, to develop good moral character. In 1837 an article was published forbidding swaddling and "overdressing in 'caps, hats, bonnets, cravats, pelisses, frills, muffles, gloves, ribands, and other paraphernalia.' "[10]

Strong morals and healthy bodies needed more freedom in which to grow. George Washington and Benjamin Franklin were mentioned as exemplars of the high virtue that can result from the "right to creep." Excessive pinning was thought harmful. Simplicity was recommended to avoid encouraging the child to put too much faith in "expensive deceiving ornaments" and thereby losing "directness of character."

Thus, the strictures of an ancient custom were finally discarded. Modern thought holds to the theory that swaddling interferes with the baby's muscular development. If the infant cannot stretch and wiggle, his limbs become weak from disuse. Some practitioners still recommend swaddling for a limited time as a treatment for a fussy baby. It is interesting to note that if the baby is folded and wrapped in the position in which it was carried in the uterus—either left leg over right or vice versa—it will stop crying.

Swaddling cloths were the original bedclothes for children, the precursors of crib quilts. Although generally discarded long ago, this centuries-old tradition of swaddling must have lived on somewhere in our unconscious. The extent of the awesomely skillful handwork, the patience, and devotion so evident in exquisitely made crib quilts, particularly in the nineteenth century, reminds us of the compelling, instinctive need to wrap the infant, to surround him with soft, reassuring warmth. It is a fact that as the custom of swaddling faded, the fashion of making beautiful crib quilts grew. Although many utilitarian crib quilts undoubtedly were hurriedly stitched together, the most beautiful—those whose function was more decorative than utilitarian—are the ones that have survived. The delicate finery of such quilts as the Bird appliqué chintz cutout (fig. 19) was never intended for everyday use; it is hard to imagine putting so fragile a piece near a baby. More likely, the quilt is a symbol: an expression of encircling, protective love, a statement of one's desire to comfort, to stop an infant's crying. Additionally, in the accomplishment of creating such an intensely personal, symbolic gift, the maker must have received in turn a measure of joy and calm for herself in the celebration of newborn life.

CHANGING VIEWS OF THE CHILD

Historically, attitudes toward children have not always been so full of tenderness. In fact, the social history of the evolution of children shows drastic changes in the way people have regarded children through the centuries. These changing attitudes are significant because they are reflected in the adult's treatment of the child: how he is raised, schooled, trained, and what he is given and is expected to produce in the area of material goods. According to Anita Schorsch's *Images of Childhood*, our views of children have undergone stupefying transformations, from the "lower animal" of the Middle Ages to the "curly dimpled lunatic" of the nineteenth century, to the principle source of innocence and hope today.[11]

Children in the Middle Ages shared about the same status as domestic animals and also the accompanying filth and pestilence. The child was sent out to a wet nurse, and, when barely old enough, was expected to work for the common good of the estate or community. He was considered expendable and easily replaced, because women, considered to be little more than breeders, could always produce more babies.[12]

A sympathetic hand, however, was extended by the previously mentioned Paolo Bagellardo, who wrote in the fifteenth century of the infant as "a human being imploring your help," and strongly suggested nursing specifically by the mother, lest the infant be "ruined by numberless diseases" from a wet nurse. He implored the mother to "Let the child love thee as a mother because of all that gentle nurture and suckling; that he, your own child, may regard you forever as his mother, and not sink, as he often does, into the child of a stranger." [13]

Children began to appear among accumulated household objects in portraits of the sixteenth century. Dutch artists even portrayed them as valued individuals in the developing family household, a significant departure from ancient views.[14]

Johann Wittich, a European physician born in 1537, wrote a book on the diseases of children in which he referred to children at one point as "poor little worms," although he later amended that by calling them "dear little children . . . the fairest of all God's creatures." [15]

According to Schorsch, the family unit as we know it was not traditional until the seventeenth century. The child was now regarded as a "little wond'rous miniature of man," "an embryo angel," and "an infant fiend." Nursed by a stranger, he was again separated and "put out" at the age of eight or nine to be apprenticed to a trade. There was no danger of the parents being tempted to love him too much.[16]

Jean Jacques Rousseau, in his eighteenth-century writings on the conditions of children, helped to free them from a cheerless existence by emphasizing their innocence and perfection, which were worthy of the respect of their parents.

The nineteenth century saw the child as being "good" or "bad." The worst enemy of the child was idleness, and his only salvation was to make himself useful, often by working in a factory. The child was expected to be a small adult, basing his moral character on his parents' model, and becoming a sturdy, worthwhile being principally through his productivity.[17]

It was not until the age of Sigmund Freud that we were again allowed to see the child as a source of goodness and optimistic expectancy, as more than just a potentially proficient laborer.

Sociologists feel that a society's attitude toward its young reveals much about itself in the areas of moral principles and stages of enlightenment. Although we must depend on societal experts and historians for precise interpretation, all of us can learn something about these aspects of society—and thus, ourselves— by exploring child-oriented folk art. From the very plain, simple patchwork crib covers to the finely appliquéd and stuffed spreads illustrated in the pages ahead, we see reflected a strong need to sustain in some form a link to the child, the embodiment of innocence and optimism.

ENGLISH AND WELSH ORIGINS

The history of American bedcoverings for children is deeply rooted in English styles. There are many similarities, although, until the middle of the nineteenth century, American styles lagged behind for a number of years while the country struggled with more basic needs. When the Colonists did get around to creating decorative objects for use in the home, they often lacked the skill and materials of their contemporaries in Europe. We can look to the inventories of our European ancestors to discover the forerunners of household possessions in America.

One of the earliest references to a child's bed quilt appears in an inventory of furniture from the Middle Ages at the Priory in Durham in northern England. Dated 1416, the list includes a child's quilt having the four corners embroidered with the symbols of the evangelists Matthew, Mark, Luke, and John.[18] It was in the same century, incidentally, that the earliest known bed quilt still surviving was made. This is a Sicilian quilt padded with wool and elaborately quilted in scenes from the legend of Tristan. In Henry VIII's reign, during the sixteenth century, cradle quilts were popular needlework projects among fashionable ladies and are listed in inventories of that period.[19] In 1551 an inventory in Wales belonging to Edward, the last feudal baron of Powys, lists as follows: "In the New Chamber over ye Garden . . . Item a quylte of redd sylke in the Nursery." [20]

Although it was less of a tradition in Wales, the use of cradle quilts has a long history in England. English crib quilts were often alternating strips of solid colors and prints, or two prints in different colors, using leftovers from full-size quilts. Baskets and Bricks were among the patterns popular in small English patchwork. Stuffedwork is found in several examples of English crib quilts, indicating a high level of craftsmanship.[21] Most quilts began their lives full size; as they began to wear out, some were cut down to cradle size, and eventually to doll size.

The Victoria and Albert Museum in London has in its collection of textiles several important early examples of small quilted spreads, forerunners of the elegant, finely stitched crib quilts found in America more than a century later. One is a linen coverlet made in England in 1703, quilted with a white cotton backing in running stitches, with silk embroidery. Another coverlet, made in the first half of the nineteenth century, is quilted linen with yellow silk. A third example from the same period in England was done in linen damask, quilted with white thread in back and running stitches and embroidered with silk in punchwork. None of these decorative spreads measures more than 40 inches in width or length.[22]

The cradle quilts of Wales were often bright cotton prints, occasionally with "frills." However, they were made very rarely, because from 1770 to around 1900 they were considered much less important than big quilts or quilted petticoats and skirts. Although no small quilt frames have been found in Wales, some quilters interviewed there in the 1950s recalled seeing them seventy to eighty years before but assumed they had subsequently been discarded. They described some frames as being a yard or a yard and one half long, but not used much until the 1930s when the demand for what they called "cot" quilts revived. From 1900 to 1930 quilters made big quilts almost exclusively. A market called the Rural Industries Bureau was organized but found it difficult at first to meet the demand for small quilts done in scale. Its clientele was mainly Londoners who, having once preferred the popular narrow-strip crib quilts, had changed their tastes to scaled-down versions of large quilt patterns. Seeing the need for more variety, the bureau asked local carpenters to build small frames. Several women reported that their grandmothers had quilted without a frame, making do with the kitchen table for a surface upon which to lay out the quilt. It was then weighed down with flatirons or stones. This primitive method resulted in crude, designless quilting in generally inferior spreads.[23]

AMERICAN CRIB QUILTS

To learn of the possessions found in American households of the 1600s, as well as the greater part of the following 100 years, we must rely on somewhat incomplete inventories, many of which were filed according to law. "Pilgrim Possessions,"[24] a manuscript at the Historic Deerfield Library in Massachusetts, stresses the difficulty in accurately tracing the possessions of the early Colonists because everyday items were taken for granted by the early settlers of the period from 1620 to 1640, certain things were forgotten altogether, and dates are hard to verify. Rural Household Inventories,[25] an assemblage of wills dating from 1675 to 1775, also suggests that these lists may not be complete because all items were not considered to be valuable enough to itemize and things belonging to someone outside the household may have been withheld from the list. However, these inventories reveal

primary information on early Colonial life and are extremely interesting historical documents.

One of the earliest references to bedcovers for children in the Plymouth Colony is found in a listing of the estate of William Palmer, Jr., August 25, 1636: "Bedding: 2 blankets, Cotes [dress or doublet], sleises [probably separate sleeves], for a childe."[26]

An estate belonging to the late Mr. John Bowles of Roxbury, Massachusetts, dated March 30, 1691, included "2 small Remnants of homespun cloth, and a

4. Pine bed in a child's room at Ashley House, Historic Deerfield. New England. Nineteenth century. H. 25″, W. 32⅛″, L. 30½″. The outstanding details of this red-painted bed, with a scalloped headboard dovetailed to the posts and the mushroom-type finials of the post tops at the foot, demand a coverlet made with equal care and quality of workmanship. Photograph courtesy Historic Deerfield, Inc., Deerfield, Massachusetts.

wicker cradle."[27] We can assume, as items were listed by rooms, with accessories grouped according to the furniture with which they were used, that these pieces of cloth were rather humble bedcovers for the cradle. Other inventories of the period include such items as "remnants of linen, cloth," and many of the households had a trundle bed with bedding "thereto belonging." The scarcity of cloth is clearly illustrated by this and numerous other individual listings of "peeces" of cotton, calico, and remnants.

One fascinating reference from the estate of Lieutenant Philip Curtice of Roxbury, Massachusetts, who died in the "honorable service of ye country," dated November 9, 1675, reads "an old rugg, a cradle, pillows and foure cushions" listed together with "one cradle rugg."[28]

American bed rugs, with the design covering the whole spread, worked in wool on homespun linen, and usually initialed and dated by their makers, are very rare. Even rarer, if they exist now at all, are bed ruggs made specifically for cradles or cribs.

The estate of the Honorable Colonel William Tailer, Esq., of Dorchester, recorded August 29, 1732, listed under "In the Children's Chamber": "2 quilts, 4 blankets, 1 small Rugg, and 2 feather beds." [29] The quilts may have been for summer, the heavier rugg for winter.

John Hayward of Roxbury, Massachusetts, died July 29, 1695. Among his possessions were "3 child's blankets" listed under the heading, "Kitchen Chamber." [30] Blankets were the bedding item most frequently listed in a number of early New England inventories, in colors of red, blue, yellow, or white, with plenty of pillows and pillowcases.

References in the *Deerfield Probate Inventories, 1743–44,* specify "coverlids" with green and red checks, one with wide stripes, and one white blanket, all of which would have been woven pieces. Listed with these items are trundle beds, cradles, a child's highchair, woolen sheets, an old quilt, a "bedquilt," and cotton pillowcases, all apparently belonging to the children of the house. Incidentally, one old quilt was valued at approximately ten percent of the price of a cow listed elsewhere in the belongings. In 1725 "old quilts" begin to appear with frequency in the estate listings.

On May 24, 1756, a list of possessions belonging to the late Joseph Warren of Roxbury was filed, including, "1 silk quilt, child's chair" and "1 pair silk christening blankets." [31]

The first Sunday after the birth of a Puritan child, the unlucky infant was wrapped in linen, covered with a christening blanket, removed from his New England home by the midwife, and whisked off to the meetinghouse to be baptized. The Puritans considered baptism to be of utmost importance, perhaps even more important than birth. Bitter cold winters made the unheated churches a deadly receiving place, where it has been recorded that, upon occasion, the christening bowl was covered with a sheet of ice that had to be broken for the ritual. Infant immersion under such circumstances presented a formidable health hazard, not to mention the potential for grave psychological consequences from being lowered into icy waters in the middle of winter. The Puritan mind-set did not concern itself with such matters; birth trauma and the subsequent difficulties of adjustment had not yet been recognized.

The Puritans stoically disregarded the raw winter weather when carrying out their religious duties. Judge Samuel Sewall wrote in his diary on January 22, 1694: "A very extraordinary Storm by reason of the falling and driving of the Snow. Few women could get to the Meeting. A child named Alexander was baptized in the afternoon." In an earlier entry he wrote of his son, Stephen, who, when he was baptized at the age of four days on a "freezing" day, "shrank at the

water but Cry'd not." Another child of this devout Puritan was baptized on a "Sabbath day, rainy and stormy . . ." Judge Sewall had fourteen children; most of them died in infancy, and only three outlived him. [32]

While woven-wool christening blankets were widely used, wealthier Pilgrims preferred the English- and European-style silk christening blankets. One belonging to Governor William Bradford (1590–1657) of Plymouth Colony was red, the color favored by royalty, with embroidered flowers. Other examples in affluent households were personalized with embroidered initials or emblems, or phrases such as "God Bless the Babe." [33] The *Boston News-Letter,* on September 5, 1765, published a list of furnishings belonging to Governor Hutchinson, which included "rich embroidered christening Blankets, Sleeves, Cradle, Quilt and Curtain, and a set of Child-bed linen."

Few of these exist today, although one fine example, a small blue spread, made around 1800 of French or Chinese silk, may be viewed at Old Sturbridge Village, Sturbridge, Massachusetts. Because of its excellent condition, we may assume it was used only on rare ceremonial occasions and became a family heirloom. It is particularly reminiscent of calamanco and linsey-woolsey spreads. The linsey-woolsey style, with a quilted background that makes the main design stand out, appears to have had a direct influence on the fine silk and satin christening spreads. *The American Heritage Dictionary of the English Language* defines *linsey-woolsey* as "a coarse fabric of cotton or linen woven with wool." Derived from the Middle English *lynsy wolsye,* the "lynsey" comes from the village in England where the fabric originated, Lindsay. Inventories rarely referred to it, and then only for clothing and petticoats. The linsey-woolsey was usually all one color with elaborate quilting designs of baskets of flowers, feathered wreaths, pineapples, or many other motifs, bordered by a distinctive framing design. This was also true of calamanco spreads, which had the additional characteristics of being shiny and having a fine weave. These bedcovers, often quite large, very closely resemble in style and effect the rich, polished, ornately handsome silk or satin crib quilt executed in diminutive proportions.

SLEEPING ARRANGEMENTS

To determine how the various sizes of crib quilts evolved, we should investigate the sleeping accommodations for children from America's early days. By doing so, we also learn much of changing social conventions, as well as the economic conditions of the American family.

Sleeping arrangements for children have varied

widely in American homes through the years. Various pieces of furniture used specifically for infants included woven baskets, arks (made somewhat like a box), cribs, some of which were mounted on rockers, and others made with turned spindles in the style of Windsor chairs.

In the past, it was acceptable for children to sleep in the same room, even in the same bed, as the servants or parents. That the custom of room or bed sharing continued well into the nineteenth century in some households is evidenced by an entry dated August 27, 1841, in the diary of Eliza Babcock Leonard, Greenfield, Massachusetts:

> Last night the nurse laid down and placed the child upon her breast and fell asleep—and turning over rolled her off the bed onto the floor, a height of about three feet. The noise of the fall together with her cries awoke all in the house. She soon became quiet and on examining her person not the slightest bruise or injury would be discovered. She was probably protected from harm by the thick covering of blankets, in which she was inwrapped.[34]

Incidentally, having survived that mishap, the child also managed to endure her own christening ceremony on Sunday, October 24, at noon.

Ironically, this was in the same year, 1841, that educator and social reformer Catharine Beecher published her first treatise with advice for the inexperienced housewife. Subsequently expanded and titled *The American Woman's Home*, the new editions were co-authored by the spinster's famous—and married mother of seven—sister, Harriet Beecher Stowe. On the subject of who sleeps where, she said:

> It is better for both mother and child, that it should not sleep on the mother's arm at night, unless the weather be extremely cold. This practice keeps the child too warm . . . A crib beside the mother, with plenty of warm and light covering, is best for the child; but the mother must be sure that it is always kept warm.[35]

A quilt, lightweight and yet providing warmth, fits the prescription perfectly. We can observe an increase in crib-quilt making from this time to the end of the nineteenth century, perhaps partly due to the influence of such voices as the Beecher sisters. Of course, it may be that we find more crib quilts from this era simply because more quilts in general have survived from this period onward.

During the seventeenth century second-story chambers were not used as sleeping quarters for families or heads of families, according to a diary entry by the Reverend William Bentley of Salem on October 29, 1812.[36] This left the upstairs for other uses, or for children to sleep there, alone.

When the layout of houses began to change from the traditional central-chimney house to a plan containing a wide center hallway, and formality in furnishings increased, the second and third stories of larger homes were often used for sleeping quarters, forcing the servants to sleep in the kitchen or attic. The 1761 inventory of a house built in Boston by Dr. Thomas Bulfinch reveals several things about how sleeping was arranged in the three-story structure. The bedding listings appear to have been for the second and third floors only, with no mention of the downstairs being used for sleeping. Three of the four second-floor chambers were listed with presumably full-size bedding and bedsteads. The third floor lists five chambers, two with no mention of bedding, two with bedsteads, and one chamber with a "Crib." [37]

Laura Russell, a New Englander born in 1827, wrote her childhood remembrances. The original manuscript, written in the 1890s, is now at Pilgrim Hall in Plymouth, Massachusetts:

> In those days children were not kept in a nursery as now, and during the winter the cradle stood in the "Sitting room," the baby at the end of the evening being taken from its warm depths, rolled in a blanket, carried to a fireless chamber and laid in a cold bed.[38]

Numerous listings of cradles appear in eighteenth-century inventories. The New-York Historical Society listing of possessions belonging to John Hebon, dated 1727, includes "one cradle" with a "small bundle child linnen . . . and two cradle blanketts." In Brookheaven [sic], New York, a list dated 1729–1730, belonging to Thomas Helme, itemizes "one creadel" with "2 childrens blancits." A listing for Monmouth Purdy of Rye, New York, in 1743 includes "one small bed, with a Rugg and one sheet," and a Westchester listing for Ryke Lent dated May 3, 1732, includes, succinctly, "The bedd and bedding the children lay upon . . ." without further details.

5. Cradle. c. 1820. New York State. H. 20″, W. 13″, L. 34″. Loving hands were beautifully carved on this unique cradle by the unknown maker. Found with its original finish, this extraordinary cradle embodies the bold spirit of folk art at its most imaginative. Photograph courtesy Grace and Elliot Snyder.

Fifty-two years later, another inventory from the same county lists several bedding items, including "1 linen quilt" and, interestingly, "1 child's setting chair." However, we are left to guess at what the child slept on, unless it was the "under bed" also listed, which would have been pulled out at night.[39]

Cradles were often made of wood panels with a hood to shield the infant from drafts. Silver and gold were placed in the infant's hand when he was first carried upstairs to sleep, in the belief that this would increase his chances for attaining wealth and make him more upwardly mobile. As is often the case with primitive customs, there is no hard evidence of its success. However, unlike the practice of infant baptism with icy water in wintry-cold drafts, this one appears harmless enough, even quaint, and we are somewhat relieved for the young creature.

6. Windsor cradle. c. 1800. New England. L. 40¾". Green-painted pine and maple. Only a very fine crib quilt would have been displayed on this exceptional example of the cabinetmaker's craft in miniature. Photograph courtesy Greenfield Village and Henry Ford Museum, Dearborn, Michigan.

The only warmth that could be found in many houses was near the fireplace or in a bed warmed with a warming pan or a heated flatiron. We can safely assume that few homes in early America possessed the luxury of the cradle made in 1811 for Napoleon's son, the King of Rome, which featured a lining of quilted-satin upholstery.

A particularly fine example of a style more usually found in adult furniture is a Windsor cradle of around 1800 made of maple and pine and painted green. Found in New England, it is now in the collection of the Henry Ford Museum, Dearborn, Michigan.

Cots were provided for older children, some with high sides to prevent their falling out. By the middle of the nineteenth century, many cots were stored under larger beds by day, and then pulled out at night. This saved space, which was at a premium in small, crowded homes. The term *trundle* or *truckle bed* (see fig. 7) derives from the medieval custom of having body servants sleep on such a bed to guard their masters at night. Our expression "to truckle" recalls this custom and means to yield to another's will.[40]

In addition to trundle beds, older children in the family might sleep on plain beds—a simple framework that supported the mattress. These extra, makeshift beds for children or servants were hard and made of straw.[41]

The fashionable notion of an entirely separate nursery reached a high level of popularity in Victorian times. However, overly embellished nursery appointments such as some of those appearing in *Godey's Lady's Book*, an immensely successful popular magazine, verged on very poor taste. One furnishing, illustrated in an 1875 issue, is black carved wood, with a cradle of basketwork, a lining and cushions of blue silk, determinedly draped with embroidered netting curtains, and topped off with a very fancy, ornately crocheted coverlet. *Godey's* did not spare the reader a full description of how to reproduce each element of this showy masterpiece, right down to the last "Smyrna stitch" in the pastel-colored fringes.[42]

It should be pointed out that a kind of "in-between-size" quilt emerged for what we now call a three-quarter-size bed, measuring approximately forty-eight-inches wide. This bed size became popular in the first quarter of the nineteenth century and was widespread throughout Victorian times, accounting for many of

7. Trundle bed. Late eighteenth or early nineteenth century. Probably New England. Red-painted maple and pine. Cots for children to sleep on were stored under full-size beds by day to save space and then pulled out at night. Bedcovers for trundle beds were sometimes smaller versions of matching full-size pieced quilts. Photograph courtesy Historic Deerfield, Inc., Deerfield, Massachusetts.

the quilts that we cannot fit into the general categories of small or large. Although some of them were obviously intended for children, such as the Children's Primer quilt (fig. 33), most of the quilts in this size were made for use by adult members of the family or hired hands.

The refuge of the nursery disappeared as the fashion of special children's rooms declined by the 1930s, taking with it the making of so many genuinely charming objects for children. In fact the twentieth-century revival of quilting, which produced many excellent still-surviving examples, declined generally around that time. The number of crib quilts being made dwindled with this trend, and the supply of fine handmade patchwork and appliquéd children's bedcovers has never again risen to previous levels.

The myriad of sizes of old bedcovers was due, in part, to the fact that country furniture was often fashioned at home, and, thus, homemade beds were not necessarily made in a manufacturer's standard size. Other factors include the availability of supplies to the quilter, her choice of design and her method of laying it out, all resulting in a remarkable range of odd-sized quilts in varying proportions.

LEARNING TO SEW

The making of quilts, especially crib quilts, was but one of several useful activities that provided a highly satisfying outlet for our historical need to be industrious, to avoid the hellish pitfalls of idle hands. Usefulness as the essence of happiness was the watchword of home life by the middle of the nineteenth-century.

In the late seventeenth and early eighteenth centuries, both boys and girls were taught at "dame schools," with the girls' curriculum having an emphasis on skills useful in the home. Spinning, knitting, and weaving were taught along with cooking. Even small children could earn money spinning and knitting simple items such as stockings by selling them to shops. Fine embroidery was done by New England schoolgirls. Quilt piecing in numerous designs was also taught. The Puritan children's education was never without its religious elements. One wonders if they all felt like a New England boy named Tony Lumpkin who got "tired of having good dinged into 'em." [43]

Girls in school in the nineteenth century also learned sewing, knitting, and related skills as well as "reading, writing, arithmetic, the elements of English grammar and geography." They learned to make "dresses, both plain and ornamented, hats, some of decoration, shirts, in many instances very neat, and others with fashionable neatly made (in miniature) beds, pillows, bolsters, and etc. with cases, curtains, patchwork, pincushions, etc." [44]

In 1808 one young worker, Mary Aycock, completed a remarkable spread at the age of fourteen years. Described in an article in The Magazine *Antiques* (July 1936) as a "Georgia miss in her 'teens,'" she is reported to have produced an intricate white counterpane from materials she created with her own hands. As if sentenced to two years of hard child labor, she, within that period of time, carded the cotton; spun the thread; wove the cloth; designed the elaborate embroidery pattern, which consisted of circles, scrolls, horns of plenty, a variety of flowers, and a vine border; and then completed the extensive project all by herself. Over a dozen types of stitchery went into the spread, which she finished off with the flourish of a homewoven fringe. It is interesting to note that the twentieth-century author of the article, writing 128 years later, commented that if such diligence can produce so important a piece of handwork, then perhaps child labor—"*in limited applications*" (author's emphasis)—is not so bad after all. If one wonders at this being judged a case of "limited application," then at least we have some idea of just how deep our roots go in the soil of the hard-work ethic.

Incidentally, perhaps further to extol the agreeable consequences of such energetic endeavor, we are told Ms. Aycock was wed shortly after completing her two-year undertaking and, "in due course, became the mother of a considerable family."

"The importance of needlework as a branch of female education" was described by Florence Hartley in her *Ladies' Handbook of Fancy and Ornamental Work* (1859):

She cannot but regard it as essential to a woman's happiness, not less than her usefulness, in accomplishing this mission of her life. If Providence has placed her in a humble or middle station of life, the ability to use her needle *with skill* in useful or ornamental work, enables her greatly to promote the well being and comfort of her family, and to gain and preserve that peace of mind which results from the consciousness of being useful. If she is placed in a more elevated station, her leisure hours may be passed, not only with profit, but with pleasure, in executing those beautiful fabrics of the needle, which contribute so largely to the adornment of her person and her dwelling . . . Fortunately for American ladies, the use of the needle in this country is fashionable in all the wealth of life; and those who are ignorant of it, whether they are aware of the fact or not, are condemned by the public sentiment of society. [45]

With this all-consuming desire to make fruitful use of time and skills, it is not surprising that the same needlework techniques employed in crib-quilt making were useful in creating a varied and sometimes odd assortment of related textile articles, such as patch-

8. Candlewick pillow sham. Dated 1832. New York State. 29½" x 61½". Made by (or for) Anne D. Miller. Patriotic motifs are enthusiastically worked into this remarkable example of candlewick embroidery. Collection of Jay Johnson: America's Folk Heritage Gallery.

work pockets (fig. 163), appliqué and pieced pillow shams (figs. 139 and 141), crewel-embroidered christening blankets (fig. 126), appliqué table covers (fig. 132), and even an appliqué rug (fig. 136). It was only natural that the needleworker should want to vary her projects, to relieve the monotony that quilting must have been at times, and to make inventive use of her skills by applying them to other small forms, such as the admirable candlewick pillow sham (fig. 8) and the equally fine stuffed-work pillow sham (fig. 9), which display traditional white work at its most refined. All of these enchanting textile pieces share in common one or more of the techniques used in quilting, whether it is simply the use of discarded scraps, types of materials, design motifs, complex stitchery patterns, or the method of construction. Each is an individual piece that transcends a merely utilitarian function to become a decorative, meaningful example of folk art done in small scale.

Quilting involved women of all ages and families; no one who could ply her needle was left out. An Autograph quilt made in Massachusetts for Paul Blackmur after the Civil War has one block inscribed: "Little Nancy Worth, aged 6 years and 6 months." [46]

Until industrial manufacturing began to supply what was previously made in the home, little girls as young as three years old were taught to sew. Catharine Esther Beecher in her *Treatise on Domestic Economy, for the Use of Young Ladies at Home and at School* (1855) wrote:

Every girl should be taught to do the following kinds of stitch, with propriety. Over-stitch, hemming, running, felling, stitching, backstitch and run, buttonhole-stitch, chain-stitch, whipping, darning, gathering, and cross-stitch. [47]

A very small child would sew with unknotted thread at first, then practice regular stitches by counting threads on a scrap of material.

Next, the simplest patchwork pattern of all was attempted, the Four-Patch (fig. 24), then the common Nine-Patch (fig. 10), then, on to variations, such as the more difficult curvilinear patterns of Melon Patch (fig. 151) and Robbing Peter to Pay Paul. Repairing old quilts was, and still is, another good way to refine skillful handling of the needle.

Each child pieced together quilt tops, traditionally at least a dozen, for her trousseau or hope chest, with the thirteenth being a special "bridal quilt." When her engagement was announced, a quilting bee or party was held, and all the ladies around came and quilted her quilt tops. Crib quilt tops were not generally counted in this traditional baker's dozen, although, as numerous unquilted tops exist, they may have been among the trousseaus of young ladies who did not marry.

Lydia Maria Child, who in the subtitle to the *American Frugal Housewife* (1838) dedicated her writing "to those who are not ashamed of economy," thought

it is very silly to tear up large pieces of cloth, for the sake of sewing them together again. But little girls often have a great many small bits of cloth, and large remnants of time, which they don't know what to do with; and I think it is better for them to make

9. Stuffed-work pillow sham (one of a pair). First half of nineteenth century. 24" x 17". The central heart is richly framed with flowers and grapevines in this beautifully crafted piece. Collection of Gail van der Hoof and Jonathan Holstein.

10. Nine-Patch variation. Mid-nineteenth century. Pennsylvania. 37½″ x 38″. One of the most admirable talents of some nineteenth-century quilters was the ability to choose and arrange fabrics in a harmonious and totally pleasing design.

cradle quilts for their dolls, or their baby brothers, than to be standing around, wishing they had something to do.[48]

Godey's Lady's Book (January 1835) informed its readers that "Little girls often find amusement in making patchwork quilts for the beds of their dolls, and some even go so far as to make cradle quilts for their infant brothers and sisters."

THE MAKERS

Whole families and their neighbors joined in the quilting, as can be seen in a painting by John Lewis Krimmel (1813, oil on canvas, now in The Henry Francis du Pont Winterthur Museum) titled *Quilting Frolic.* A large family could be "kept out of idleness, and a few shillings saved" by participating in the quilting.[49]

The Beecher sisters thought that boys should learn the arts of

mending their own garments and aiding their mothers or sisters in the kitchen, with great skill and adroitness; and at an early age, they usually very much relish joining in such occupations. The sons of such mothers, in their college life, or in roaming

about the world, or in nursing a sick wife or infant, find occasion to bless the forethought and kindness which prepared them for such emergencies. Few things are in worse taste than for a man needlessly to busy himself in women's work; and yet a man never appears in a more interesting attitude than when, by skill in such matters, he can save a mother or wife from care and suffering.[50]

This "interesting attitude" was later endorsed by Mary Schenck Woolman who, in the early twentieth century, was considered to be a progressive teacher. "In the first three or four years . . . it is well for the boys and the girls to be taught the same kinds of handwork. Experience has proved that boys are greatly interested in sewing when it is connected with their pursuits . . ." [51]

At the age of ten Calvin Coolidge pieced a Baby's Blocks quilt, and Dwight D. Eisenhower and his brother worked with their mother on her quilts.

People convalescing in hospitals and at home, people serving jail sentences, people isolated in their rural homes for long, cold winters, all quilted to avoid the boredom and anxiety of idle loneliness. Never should the needle be considered an emblem of drudgery.

It is interesting to give some thought to how the prolific quilters of our past, particularly the young ones themselves, felt about the powerful voices of educators and social reformers, whose sermonizing on the virtues of usefulness prodded their hands ever onward. For insight, we turn to the humble diaries kept by industrious young girls. Although the authors of these diaries discreetly hid many of the personal feelings that they must have had in their prim, disciplined lives, they offer us information on the various activities of their days, and, upon occasion, do reveal emotions—the tensions, joys, and strains of enduring life when America was a struggling new country.

One example of a diligent young soul is found in the Diary of Elizabeth Fuller, 1791, of Princeton, Massachusetts. The young lady made daily entries in her diary consisting of how much work she had accomplished, such as how many skeins of yarn she had spun that day. Numerous references to spinning, picking, washing, carding, weaving, and making various articles of clothing of linen and wool are recorded. On May 3, 1791, she wrote, "I wove two and an half yards. Got out the piece, there is thirty one yards and an half; have finished my weaving for this year. I have woven a hundred and forty yards since the ninth of March."[52] This unending work was interrupted only by weekly visits to church on the Sabbath to hear sermons on such things as the "wages of sin." Judging from the amount of work she did, including making several items of clothing and even quilting a whole coat on June 22, little time or energy was left to contemplate the preacher's cautionary advice.

In the diaries of Sally and Pamela Brown for 1832 through 1838, Plymouth Notch, Vermont, we find innumerable references to the sewing and handiwork of two very industrious sisters.[53]

Feb. 1832

17, Fri. Worked about the house until half past twelve. Began to spin worsted. Spun ten knots.

18, Sat. Did some chores. Spun 12 knots.

20, Tues. Did the house work, sewed some. I twisted 12½ knots worsted.

Tues, 21st. Worked about the house. Spun 11½ knots worsted. In the evening doubled what I had spun.

27, Mon. Worked some about the house and made my waist.

Mar. 4, I have neglected this journal since Tuesday. Have been employed sewing, knitting about the house.

As the diaries continued, the girls

made a cape for Pamela . . . began to make a cape bonnet for Susan . . . began a bonnet for myself . . finished knitting George's stockings . . . finished James' pantaloons . . . began a spencer for George . . . Spun, doubled and twisted 20 knots of stocking yarn . . . Began to make a cape for Mother . . . began to piece a bed quilt out of two old calico gowns . . . began a pair of double mittens . . . quilted the lining to my cloak . . . worked upon Susan's woolen gown . . . Sewed with Louisa upon Thomas' pantaloons . . . knit a cap for old Mrs. Hall.

Within the period of April 8 through April 29, 1835, Pamela "Made Thomas a shirt . . . began another shirt for Thomas . . . Began a night gown . . . made me a night cap too . . . tied a comfortable . . . quilted a bed quilt . . . made me a night gown . . . we quilted Susan a petticoat."

Other items made by Miss Brown include "a cloak, silk work bag, petticoat, pair of pillow cases, paper window curtains, a needle book, thread case, a (tamboured) lace bag, a pair of corsets, mittens." On Wednesday, May 10, 1835, Miss Brown and a friend "pieced a small quilt," presumably a child's quilt.

A curious story appeared in the diary of Anna Green Winslow on April 18, 1772, about a trade arrangement involving a patchwork quilt that, although intended to be a full-size bridal quilt when complete, ended up smaller.

Some time since I exchang'd a piece of patchwork, which had been wrought in my leisure intervals, with Miss Peggy Phillips, my schoolmate, for a pair of curious lace mitts with blue flaps which I shall send, with a yard of white ribbin edg'd with green to Miss Nancy Macky for a present. I had intended that the patchwork should have grown large enough to have cover'd a bed when that same live stock which you wrote me about some time since, should

be increas'd to that portion you intend to bestow upon me, should a certain event take place.[54]

In the 1830s Laura Russell recalled the hardships of growing up in Plymouth, Massachusetts.

It was not uncommon to see the frost sparkle on our yellow-washed chamber walls, and we frequently had to break the ice in our pitchers before we could perform our hasty and limited morning ablutions. I have since heard my brother say that he often came home from school with stockings soaked with snow-water, sat through the evening without changing them, and put them on the next morning frozen still. A striking example of the survival of the toughest, if not of the fittest.

She describes the school which served as "a sort of day nursery" taught by "an old dame whom we always addressed as Marm." Children entered the school at about two years of age and remained for several years before graduating to a "private school of higher grade."

The great Bible lay upon a table under the looking-glass between the windows and, with the Old Farmer's Almanac, constituted the old lady's entire library. On the sacred volume and the almanac was a small wooden box into which at the close of each day we dropped our little brass thimbles and our bit of patchwork with its irregular, blackened stitches piled one upon another after having been many times picked out and re-sewed with squeaking, crooked needle and tear-dimmed eyes.[55]

The heavy sorrow suffered by American families because of the high rate of infant mortality, which prevailed until after 1850, is recorded in the diary of a housewife in Maine. In September 29, 1815, Sarah Connell Ayer began keeping a journal again, following a four-year interruption in her daily writing. In the simple, matter-of-fact style in which so many diaries of the day were written, she states that since her last journal ended October 26, 1811, she had given birth to and buried four children in as many years.

Since closing my last journal, I have been the mother of four children, which now lay side by side in the graveyard. The first was born in 1811, Dec. 10th. The second the 10th of Oct. 1812, and lived only two days, the third the 4th of Sept. 1813, and the 4th, the 25th of Nov. 1814. This last was a sweet, interesting boy, and lived to be six months old. He was a lovely flower, and I trust he is now transplanted in the garden of Heaven. Though the death of this child was a great trial, yet I hope I was made to bow submissive to the will of my Heavenly Father.[56]

In the nineteenth century the average family had five to nine children, born two years apart. One-fifth of that number died within two years of birth. It may be that we find more crib quilts made after 1850 because of the decline in infant deaths.

Although quilting has always been closely associated with the joys of life, the craft was not forgotten in times of sorrow. One account of homesteading in rural West Texas in the 1920s describes a quilting bee held for the purpose of making a quilt and a quilted lining for the casket of a neighbor's baby who had died. This casket quilt was made of fine blue silk to cover the baby. The women spent a day on the quilt, while the men made the casket.[57]

This same affectionate remembrance of times past describes learning to quilt as a child. One of a poor family of nine children, Patricia Cooper's mother had encouraged her to learn gardening and other useful skills as a practical matter. The author's first quilt was a Flower Garden in flowered prints, chosen because of the child's fondness for flowers. She was taught how to pick cotton of high quality for the batting, and to clean and card it into pieces about twelve by five inches. These were then laid on the backing and covered by the quilt top, ready to take to the quilting bee. While she was still too young to quilt, she was assigned needle threading to keep a constant supply ready for the quilters. She recalls her brother quilting with the whole family, and even her husband, who pieced a quilt at age six during a bout with the measles, joining in by helping to cut pieces. The first time the young Ms. Cooper was allowed to quilt with her mother, she was too short to sit in a chair and reach the frame, so she stood next to her mother, awkwardly working her needle, despite discouraging remarks from her father. It was a moment of great pride and meaning to the girl, who, like generations of children before her, dreamed of quilting as well as her highly skilled mother.

Another fond childhood memory of quilting is brief but amusing:

> The children played around and under the porch and tried to listen to the ladies talk . . . the children never really understood much of the conversation because just as the ladies got to the interesting point they would whisper . . . The children were invaluable at these quilting bees. They were stationed below the quilting frames to return the needles after the ladies stuck them down through the quilt.[58]

Crib quilts are by their very nature personal. They call forth emotional responses from us when we look at and touch them, and our sensibilities are stirred to wonder at what creative impulses and emotional needs must have gone into their making. Pursuing the idea that crib quilts have played a significant part in the emotional lives of their makers and their families will help us to grasp better the context from which some of these remarkable objects emerged. We can also sympathize with the maker's attempts to express her creativity, as well as other desires, such as can be found in the following story.

It concerns an eccentric upstate New York spinster, Old Maid Smith, and gives us one idea of how some crib quilts came to remain unused. Known in her village as "queer," the woman was a hermit whose only intercourse with the members of the community was in the rare shopping visit to the village stores. She was well known for a stinging tongue and a particular hostility toward men. A feared and hated figure, she became an isolated curiosity about whom her neighbors speculated for a time, eventually losing interest. One older neighbor recalled how Old Maid Smith was once a beautiful woman who, at sixteen, had withdrawn from finishing school upon the death of her mother. When her father died a year later, she dismissed the servants and became a recluse in her house for the next half century. In 1927 she was discovered dead in her yard under a tree. Her will ordered a sale of the contents of her house, and the neighbor in charge discovered, among dozens of unused lace, silk, and linen garments, drawers overflowing with beautiful, handmade infants' garments, including heavily embroidered dresses and petticoats. Among the oldest of the items was a white, unfinished crib quilt elaborately quilted in designs of pineapples, grapes, and flowers, with a Princess Feather border. No clues were uncovered in any of the woman's other belongings, such as a diary or letter, that gave any reason for the strange fashion in which she lived. Although some felt that Old Maid Smith had wasted her life indulging in morbid selfishness," one can imagine a great deal of the suffering and private torment endured by this lonely soul was stitched into the delicately sewn, never-used crib quilt.[59]

As we have seen, crib quilts have been made or at least worked on by all kinds of hands; young girls, boys, fathers, neighbors, friends, everyone. Mothers sometimes found time to make a quilt for their infants, although without assistance, these would necessarily have been simpler, more quickly done patterns. Little girls, anxious that the piecework would all work out, carefully stitched their patchwork, sometimes for a doll quilt as a practice piece. Irregular stitching and slightly out-of-line patches are found in several doll and crib quilts, indicating the makers' beginner's status. The varying sizes of the quilting stitches illustrated in figure 27, *Louisa 1851*, indicate a mild uncertainty in that area of the maker's work, whereas the piecework and appliqué appear to be on much surer footing. Whether skilled or not, the main needlework emphasis for some little girls of eight or nine was to get a good start on quilts for a hope chest in preparation for marriage. There are also many accounts of maiden aunts who lovingly stitched crib quilts and made several as baptismal gifts for godchildren.

Commercial offerings to quilters over the years

11. Stereoscopic view of a fashionably appointed nursery. 1903. A little girl learns to make a patchwork quilt, perhaps for her doll's bed or perambulator, under the loving observation of her well-fed companion. Photograph courtesy The Library of Congress, Washington, D.C.

have not always been a great source for inspired originality or creative expression. Although some examples of commercially produced, "store-bought" patterns, executed with fine workmanship, were and are quite successful, the achievement is most often a result of the quilter having injected a bit of her own imagination into the piece, by such means as rearranging the suggested colors, or reworking details of the pattern to her own satisfaction. For the quilter who does not have access to great traditional patterns handed down from generation to generation, or who does not possess the artistic ability to draw original patterns, commercial patterns have served as a reasonable alternative. All too often, however, the resulting quilt lacks individual style and imaginative spark. Mail-order specialty-store patterns are sometimes stamped on muslin, with even simple quilting stitches indicated, and packaged in kits.

One such offering in 1916, the Sunbonnet Kiddies crib quilt,[60] included pieces stamped for cutting and embroidering, with the "kiddies" dressed in outfits of pink, blue, yellow, purple, and heliotrope, with matching parasols. All aesthetic decisions were taken care of by the accompanying instructions, leaving no room whatsoever for the imagination.

Rosalie and Ona Wilkinson published a catalogue titled *Added Attractiveness in Your Bedroom* in 1922 in Ligonier, Indiana. The Wilkinson sisters had, in their catalogue's own words, the "fine artistic ability and keen vision" (not to mention the sharp eye for profit) to supply "the most beautiful quilts that human hands could make . . . the Wilkinson Art Quilts." Their baby quilts, as they called them, were sateen, filled with lamb's wool from Australia ("the finest"), and designed specifically to appeal to the owner's desire for cultural refinement to impress her peers. Unfor-

12. *Alice in Calicoland.* Signed H. B. Kile, 1975. Lake View, Iowa. 63″ x 50″. An uninhibited quiltmaker, inspired by old photographs, has created a captivating menagerie of make-believe creatures, allowing her imagination full rein. *Alice* won the coveted first-place blue ribbon at the Iowa State Fair in 1976.

tunately, although these personalized, monogrammed spreads were advertised as "original and entirely worked by hand by skilled needleworkers" in the Wilkinson's employ, the ultimate effect was more precious than charming, lacking the true artistry of the crib quilts produced by America's nonprofessionals.

The answer most often given to the question who made crib quilts is, simply, grandmothers. To find out why, we spoke to several, including Mrs. Hazel Kile of Lake View, Iowa, who won first prize at the Iowa State Fair in 1976 with the crib quilt called *Alice in Calicoland,* illustrated in figure 12.[61] The design is original, based on a picture Mrs. Kile had saved from thirty-five or forty years ago. She had always intended to make a quilt for her niece but had never had time. With the old picture in mind, she drew the figures and filled in the spaces according to her preference as she "went along." She does not feel the quilt is totally original because it is based on a picture, but her free adaptation is without question her own creation. She chose the appliqué method because it best suited her plan to re-create the animals in a "picture quilt." Her first pictorial spread was a full-size quilt made during the Bicentennial using the history of Iowa as the theme, and it included a log cabin, a buffalo, and the Little Brown Church in the Vale in a small brown-and-white-check print. She prefers appliqué when working by hand, which was the case while she wintered in Texas where she made the quilt. If a sewing machine is handy, piecework is preferred.

It is difficult to say exactly how long the crib quilt took to make, because Mrs. Kile, like many traditional quilters, was working on two other quilts simultaneously and liked to alternate the work, spreading the project out over two winters. The first winter was spent hunting up the cloth, which had been given to her by a friend in Montana, then sketching the designs on a big piece of brown wrapping paper and transferring them to the cloth. She traced the figures one inch smaller in order to lay out her plan and fit them into the space. She waited until the following winter to appliqué the figures and then sent the quilt back to Iowa to be quilted by a friend, to make sure the quilt was finished while she tended to other projects. Upon the completion of the quilting, Mrs. Kile bound the edges herself as the final step.

She is very excited about the current revival of interest in quilting, having recently attended an "elder hostel" in northern Minnesota, where she exchanged ideas with other senior citizens in a quilting class. She does not recall having crib or even full-size quilts in her home in Illinois, where she grew up, but remembers working on her first quilt in the 1930s with her mother during that decade's revival of quilting. She likes making crib quilts because they are easy to carry around, even though she works mostly on a small frame in a vacant room in her house. She recently made one crib quilt with a horse on it for her niece who is an avid rider.

Alice was made because Mrs. Kile just "wanted to do something." Two generations of children had slipped into adulthood before she had had a chance to complete it, so she decided to sell it. She does not like kits or commercial patterns because she feels they would not be personally expressive. She likes to take an idea and then "carry it out myself. If I want polka dots on the pig, I put them there. If the ears are floppy, I work it out as I go along. I draw cats like I used to." When we reached her, she was in the middle of making a "bread quilt," a twenty-inch square to cover bread dough and keep it warm while it rises. She says, "if you don't want to cover the bread with it, hang it in the kitchen as a wall hanging."

This independent spirit recalls the originality of the nonpareil quilters of a century ago, who were unafraid to try something new, to dare to be different, and who didn't give a "hoot" about conformity.

AMISH CRIB QUILTS

Among the most unusual and treasured of all crib quilts are those made before 1940 by the Amish people of Pennsylvania, Ohio, Indiana, Iowa, and other scattered areas. We asked several Amish quilters why relatively few Amish crib quilts had been made or had survived, especially in Pennsylvania where many superb full-size quilts originated. One of the more accomplished elderly quiltmakers answered simply that they made them to use, and, consequently, "used them all up." She, herself, had never seen a miniature Center Diamond quilt and remembered only one small Bars during her eighty-odd years in rural Pennsylvania, believing that such patterns were reserved mostly for full-size quilts.

Another reason that few crib quilts were made by the Old Order Amish has to do with their custom of adult baptism. The Puritans in America, regarding infant baptism as one of the most significant events of a lifetime, spent a great deal of time and creative effort preparing handmade clothing and ceremonial accessories, including christening blankets, for the event. Lacking this all-important rite, the Amish had no compelling need to produce splendid needlework for the newborn child. The examples illustrated here, then, are truly exceptional and are among the finest, most unusual crib quilts ever sewn.

In general, the Amish used only solid-color cloths, rejecting prints as being too "worldly" or "fancy." If a printed fabric was the only material available, it was grudgingly used, preferably on the back of the quilt where few would see it. Some crib quilts are impossible to authenticate as definitely of Amish origin, because of their quilters' strong affinity with the Mennonite people. Unless one knows the precise background of an Amish crib quilt through reliable information such as that provided by the family of the maker, one can only surmise its origin from certain characteristics.

The Amish chose piecework as their preferred method of quiltmaking because appliqué seemed too "fancy," and the rich quilting patterns would embellish the quilt in a more acceptable fashion. They often used surprisingly dark colors, considering that the spreads were made for infants. However, one is constantly astonished by the unpredictable range of colors in unexpected juxtaposition. The old Amish quiltmakers were bold in their choice of color combinations and were uninhibited by our modern obsession with matching or contrasting colors according to the dictates of interior decorators or women's magazines. As a result, we are free to enjoy the interplay of pink, red, blue, lavender, and black in such spirited examples as the Bear's Paw (fig. 109).

A number of Amish crib quilts were made in an array of bright colors, particularly in the midwestern settlements, such as the Philadelphia Pavement variation (fig. 120), and sometimes in combination with darker hues, such as the Old Maid's Puzzle (fig. 111). Because the materials used in Amish crib quilts were also used for clothing, we look to the Amish children's dress for an explanation of these exuberant colors. In the Amish countryside one can see cheerful hues of pink, turquoise, lavender, green, and even gold in the dresses and aprons of Amish children working in the fields and yards. An Amish mother told us that as the children grow older, they dress in darker colors, and eventually favor the somber black clothing with which we more often associate the Amish people.

Midwestern Amish quilters made extensive use of black, an unlikely color for baby quilts, perhaps to introduce seriousness to the Amish child before he or she has had much of a chance to stray. For whatever motive, be it by design or by accident, it is most effective in such examples as the simple Plain Quilt (fig. 117), which provides a dramatic, polished black background for the vivid blue inner frames that are enriched with thousands of delicately ornate quilting stitches spreading throughout this extraordinary piece.

It is surprising to note that the diligent, industrious Amish, known for their resourcefulness, did not adopt quilting as a tradition until they came to the United States. For a people who were, and still are, determined to live separately from the world around them, they have been ingenious at absorbing into the culture certain "worldly" conveniences, such as the sewing machine. Although it was always the type operated by a foot pedal, as they choose not to use electricity, the machine was used for the piecing of the majority of their quilts. The quilting, however, was almost always done by hand, and it is here that the exquisite level of workmanship was achieved. Having borrowed the idea of making quilts from their neighbors outside the community, all of whom are referred to as "English," the Amish housewives developed their own distinct style of quiltmaking, which is easily differentiated by its unusual appearance.

The earliest examples of Amish quilting we have observed date from the third quarter of the nineteenth century: the majority were made between 1890 and 1940. Few Amish crib quilts either were made or have survived from before the twentieth century. Although impractical for use with infants, wools were preferred in the earlier quilts, but as it became harder to obtain, the quilters were forced to rely on rayon, crepe, or whatever materials were available. The majority of Amish crib quilts found in Ohio and other midwestern states are of later dates, generally of the 1920s and 1930s, done in a wide range of solid-colored cottons, often with a black ground and/or border. The midwestern Amish borrowed freely from their "En-

13. Amish Checkerboard Diamond. Indiana. c. 1920. 42″ x 42″. Pennsylvania Amish quiltmakers favored the more traditional Center Diamond pattern, pieced in a solid color. However, the Amish of the Midwest were often more adventurous in experimenting with patterns, occasionally creating a unique variation such as this one.

glish" neighbors, reproducing a variety of traditional patterns, such as the Double Wedding Ring (fig. 123). However, even though the pattern is definitely not of Amish origin, the choices of colors and materials are thoroughly Amish. How many conventional quilters would execute the usually whimsical, frequently sweet and sentimental, Double Wedding Ring in startlingly bold, powerful, intense hues of purple, scarlet, and orange with stark areas of black?

An extremely rare pattern for use in old crib quilts is the Grandmother's Dream (fig. 100), which combines two of the three most-loved Amish patterns, Sunshine and Shadow enclosed in a Diamond.

Unhappily, it must be said that the workmanship nowadays is vastly inferior to that from before 1940. Much of this is caused by the lack of the fine old materials that have been replaced by modern, easy-care synthetics, as well as the fact that Amish quilts are now made mostly to sell to tourists and retailers. The same dedication and perfection that went into quilts made for their own loved ones in the early part of this century have disappeared, perhaps not surprisingly, from the commercially oriented quiltmaking of today. Harsh, gaudy, no-iron prints, quickly arranged in simple, unimaginative combinations and filled with polyester batting prevail. Most disappointing of all, the quilting stitchery is often done in a "hurry-up"

manner in order to finish the quilts quickly. These trends, all dictated by the "worldly" consumers outside the Amish community, should make us especially aware of the priceless, irreplaceable qualities of the old quilts. Most likely, we shall never again see their equal.

DOLL QUILTS FOR DOLL BEDS

The favorite toy of little girls down through the ages has always been the doll. Because a doll is the image of a human being, scaled down to a child's size, it is a more personal and cherished object than other toys. Fantasies of mother-to-child and friend-to-friend relationships can be privately explored with this mute and faithful companion.

When it came to providing clothes and furniture for a doll, parents—especially in the nineteenth century—saw a golden opportunity for their daughters to learn sewing skills and develop housewifely zeal. Catharine Beecher and her sister Harriet Beecher Stowe saw the construction of doll's things and their upkeep as practice for the future.

When a little girl begins to sew, her mother can promise her a small bed and pillow, as soon as she has sewed a patch for these; and then a bedstead, as soon as she has sewed the sheets and cases for pillows; and then a large doll to dress, as soon as she has made the undergarments; and thus go till the whole contents of the baby-house are earned by the needle and skill of its little owner. Thus the task of learning to sew will become a pleasure; and every new toy will be earned by useful exertion. A little girl can be taught, by the aid of patterns prepared for the purpose, to cut and fit all articles necessary for her cloth. She can also be provided with a little wash-tub and irons, and thus keep in proper order a complete miniature domestic establishment.[62]

To help the child learn to sew, in 1912 the S.E. Cassino Company of Salem, Massachusetts, offered *A Complete Manual of Sewing* by Mary H. Morgan, a volume instructing little girls in various stitches and showing "how to lay out patterns and . . . make a complete wardrobe for a doll."

Many a little girl learned how to make quilts by making one first for her doll, as evidenced by the sometimes irregular craftsmanship found in many doll quilts. Some children made quilts not only for their doll beds but also for their doll carriages.

In more prosperous homes dollhouses were provided, ranging from primitive specimens usually put together by the girl's father to the lavishly appointed and meticulously hand-crafted examples sold by dollhouse firms. Best & Company of New York, located at Fifth Avenue and 35th Street, in 1912, offered a large selection of dolls, doll clothes, dishes, and furniture, but presumably the child was expected to provide her own doll's bedding. Adults loved these houses also, which is probably why the fancier ones that have survived are beautifully intact: they were to look at, not play with!

The dolls in these commercially manufactured houses were designed for them and are sized in proportion to the rooms. The beds are covered with the type of bedding suited to the particular style of room. An inventory of the 1864 Fair-y Villa dollhouse of a Mr. Fair-Child of New York [63] lists a bed having "Bed canopy and curtains, mattress, pair pillows, pr. linen sheets, pr. linen pillowcases, blanket, and Marseilles Quilt." In the nursery one bed is covered with a bedspread and a Marseilles Quilt, and there is a "cradle with lace & silk curtains." Both the cook's and the waiter's rooms have quilts on the beds.

The quilts in this and many other dollhouses were sewn with great attention to detail; the emphasis was on making the doll quilt look as much as possible like a small replica of a full-size quilt, with all the usual techniques of patchwork and appliqué employed.

One remarkable room constructed by Mr. and Mrs. Frank Steele is called "The Quilting Party" [64] and shows several nineteenth-century ladies sitting around

14. Doll's four-post rope bed. c. 1840. New England. L. 16″. Nineteenth-century American doll furniture, on which a child's first efforts at piecing quilts could be displayed, was a source of endless delight to children. Photograph courtesy Betty Sterling.

a quilting frame and sewing away. The dolls, their costumes, the room, and its furnishings are all authentic period miniatures or accurately designed replicas.

The extent to which dolls and their houses have always fascinated children and adults is reflected in this quote from *To Lilliput and Brobdingnag* by Jonathan Swift (1726): "When in Brob, the first box in which he was carried about had a quilt from a doll's bed for him to lie on." Surely this is the logical extension of the dream of a tiny house so perfect one could live in it: becoming the doll oneself!

OTHER SMALL WONDERS

The pervasiveness of needlework in earlier American homes can be seen in the remarkable variety of textile objects made for them. The ever-resourceful women created other small items, in addition to the splendid crib quilts, out of a need to make use of needlework skills, idle hands, and creative energy. The odd assortment of things shown here all have in common the delightful charm deriving from the vigorous implementation of one or more techniques used in quiltmaking: piecework, appliqué, pattern motifs, or simply the recycling of worn-out clothing. They are not the products of the more formal training received at finishing schools, such as samplers or theorems, but rather have their own spontaneous reason for being. An original flair for employing traditional elements in fresh contexts enhances their enchanting quality, and they seldom fail to evoke a personal response in the viewer.

They are functional, but go beyond a mere practical usefulness. They are ingenuously imaginative, and work well in the home as decorative objects when used as wall art or in harmony with other primitive objects, and are important contributions to the decorative arts. And, like crib quilts, they are all small.

COLLECTING CRIB QUILTS

For the person interested in collecting crib quilts, it will be helpful to view firsthand as many examples of fine needlework as possible by attending museum exhibits. The Whitney Museum of American Art in New York held an exhibition from July through September 1971 that significantly increased public interest in the field, and in the spring of 1979 The Baltimore Museum of Art showed a collection composed entirely of crib and doll quilts. The Shelburne Museum in Vermont has perhaps the finest permanent collection of full-size quilts available, and many other museums throughout the country have smaller holdings. It will help to know what to look for when collecting if one is fa-

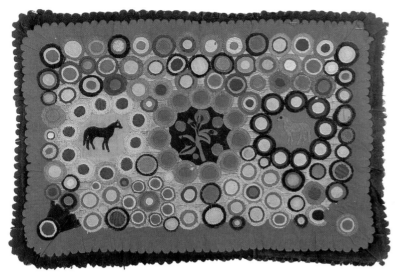

15. Table rug. Third quarter nineteenth century. New England. 22½" x 32". Small, elaborately appliquéd rugs like this example were often made for use on a table, chest, or similar flat surface. Collection of Helaine and Burton Fendelman.

miliar with the best. Keep in mind that the folk art of fine quilting as it was at its height in the nineteenth centry has, unfortunately, declined. Modern efforts, even among the Amish, rarely compare. As there is a finite number of genuine pieces, some modern quilts are being sold as antiques by unscrupulous or unknowing dealers and auction houses.

The average collector, interested in a good investment as well as a fine piece of folk art, is best advised to seek out a specialist in the specific antique, that is, crib quilts. No one dealer can be totally knowledgeable in every field of antiques, and the experience and interest of the expert can be invaluable in cases of uncertain or borderline provenance or value.

Until the middle of this century quilts were not thought of as particularly valuable, and even the best examples could be bought very cheaply, but one should remember that nowadays, for good pieces, such "bargains" no longer exist! A lot of time and trouble will be saved by buying the best from a reputable dealer at a realistic price—the best always appreciates fastest and surest. Although auctions at top houses can offer a fair certainty of authenticity, the payment of four or five times the estimated value is not uncommon. Paying tomorrow's prices for today is buying for fun, not profit. Competing at auction does not always allow for the wisest consideration in buying.

The most desirable pieces are those in fine condition and the most unusual in design, especially if the maker departed slightly from tradition and thus infused the work with personal feeling and real imagination. For authenticity, depend on the dealer and your own feelings. If a piece is misrepresented, it is usually because the dealer is in error, not dishonest. The top dealers are generally happy to give a guarantee on each piece sold.

If you have taste, you know it and should use it. If you don't, again, rely on your dealer and listen to his advice. But don't buy what you think you *should* buy. Buy what you like. If you don't like a piece at first, you probably won't grow to like it any better later, and if other people don't like it either, it won't be worth much.

The pieces illustrated here have been selected from many hundreds of quilts in the collections of private individuals, dealers, and museums to show the wide range of what we consider to be top examples. All of us wish we had bought more good crib quilts in past years when they seemed plentiful. However, even though they are now scarce, really fine examples do appear on the market from time to time and can still be found by the persistent and adventurous collector.

DISPLAYING CRIB QUILTS

Even the most expensive crib quilt, when considered as a piece of wall art, may be a bargain. The same investment would not buy a painting of comparable quality or uniqueness, and many paintings would not appreciate in value so steadily.

The simplest method of hanging a crib quilt is to hand-sew a strip of either Velcro or grosgrain ribbon on to the back top edge. Catch just the backing material with the needle, being sure not to sew clear through the quilt. If Velcro is used, simply staple a second strip exactly the same size to a strip of molding, which is then mounted on the wall. If desired, skip the molding and attach the Velcro directly to the wall. Velcro stapled directly with a staple gun is faster, if the wall is of suitable material. Then, press the quilt into place on the wall.

If preferred, sew small squares of Velcro on each of the two bottom corners, or anywhere the quilt buckles, in order to smooth out the edges. Attach corresponding pieces of Velcro to the wall and press into place. Some people put Velcro all the way around the perimeter for a very neat, stretched surface.

Going one step further, a frame resembling a canvas stretcher can be made to the exact dimensions of the quilt, with Velcro attached. Sew Velcro around the back edges of the quilt and press on the frame. This is a particularly effective way to display the crib quilt and allows for easy removal for cleaning or storage. Also, hinges in the frame allow for folding and easy moving or storage.

If grosgrain is used, sew the strip on the top of the

back to form a pocket. Slide a piece of flat molding into the pocket and attach to the wall with the sawtooth picture hangers found at framing stores.

A more permanent and expensive framing method is to use Plexiglas, but this should be done only by very experienced framers. One unlucky collector tried a bargain framer in Greenwich Village who, to make the crib quilt fit the frame, blithely cut out sections of the quilt to accommodate the frame's crosspieces. This damage seriously decreased the value of the piece. A Plexiglas box provides an elegant, more formal finish for the crib quilt and protects it from dampness and air pollutants, one of the worst of which is cigarette smoke. However, a bit of the textural charm of the quilt is lost, and an element of artificiality accompanies the pressed-behind-glass method. Ideally, the Plexiglas should not touch the textiles, if possible; although this makes the whole frame more fragile. Again, personal preference and budgetary considerations should be one's guide.

Although direct or even bright indirect light can cause fading of the more fugitive dyes (dark greens and reds from Pennsylvania are among the most common casualties), one can hardly enjoy folk art stored in a closet. Therefore, it is advisable to choose a pleasing location on a wall that does not get direct or reflected sunlight, hang the crib quilt, and inspect it regularly for signs of fading. If such signs appear, either alter the lighting or move the piece to a new location.

STORING CRIB QUILTS

Crib quilts should be out and enjoyed as much as possible, but there are times when they must be stored, perhaps for the rotation of a collection. Store them in a clean, cloth bag in a dry, moderate temperature. A blanket chest is ideal, and a closet is likewise suitable. High heat, such as that in an attic, may cause discoloration, and, naturally, severe damage is caused by leaking water, rodents, and moths, all dangers to watch for. Plastic should never be used for long periods of storage, nor should paper, unless it is the specially prepared rag-content type used by museums.

CLEANING CRIB QUILTS

Many crib quilts have been ruined by people obsessed with cleanliness, who use harsh detergents and bleaches that considerably weaken old textiles. Try to resist the temptation to achieve the "whiter whites," etc., of television commercials. Dirt can damage tex-

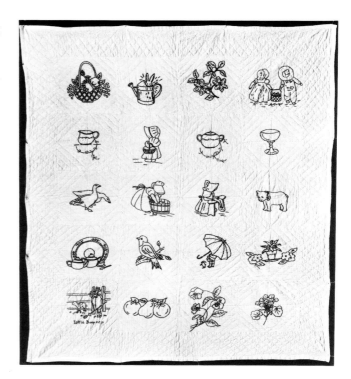

16. Embroidered picture quilt. c. 1915. Pennsylvania. 40" x 34". In the early part of this century pictures of interest to children were often embroidered in red on a white ground, then quilted for a pleasant overall effect. Collection of Lena Kaplan.

tiles when allowed to stay in the fibers, however, so cleansing is sometimes a necessity. If the piece can be washed, that is the most desirable method; however, each fabric should be tested with soap and water on a cotton swab for colorfastness. If running occurs (embroidery thread is one of the worst offenders), dry cleaning by a fine dry cleaner is recommended. Some yellowing on white muslins occurs, but, if done carefully by an experienced specialist, the safety of dry cleaning may be worth the slight alteration of appearance caused by the residue of cleaning chemicals.

For washing, a mild detergent is recommended, in some cases together with an all-color bleaching powder, which can help set the colors and whiten the white muslins. Very cold water is preferable, allowing the piece to soak facedown, so that when the quilt is handled, the back takes most of the strain of handling and the weight of the water. Gently squeeze out soapy water, rinse two or three times in clean, cold water; then, to the final rinse water, add a small amount of fabric softener, which will add fluffiness to the quilt when dry and bring out the quilting patterns. Allow to dry stretched on a flat surface of towels, or over a shower curtain rod covered with towels, changing its position often to avoid creases.

GALLERY OF CRIB QUILTS
AND
OTHER SMALL WONDERS

PIECED QUILTS

17. Whole-cloth quilt. Early nineteenth century. 25½″ x 17″. Printed floral chintzes, imported from India and Europe, were used in large sections to form decorative spreads during the last quarter of the eighteenth century through the middle of the nineteenth century. Photograph courtesy Gloria List. Collection of Kiracofe and Kile.

18. Framed Medallion quilt. Second quarter nineteenth century. Dimensions unavailable. Chintzes printed with bird and floral motifs were imported from England and India and enjoyed great popularity in nineteenth-century America. This is an unusual miniature interpretation of one of the earliest types of quilts, combining the richness of several intricate prints with a basic piecework design. Photograph courtesy Kelter-Malcé Antiques, New York. Private collection.

19. Pieced and appliquéd chintz cutout. 1830–1840. Found in New York State. 33½″ x 34″. A tiny bird perched in a blossoming Tree of Life is a cutout from fine imported chintz meticulously appliquéd to form the central medallion of this most elegant spread. Private collection.

20. Star. Second quarter nineteenth century. Massachusetts. 40″ x 33″. The fragile chintzes in this early example are pieced in a Central Star design extended into four elongated points, a logical solution for filling the rectangular space. Collection of Gail van der Hoof and Jonathan Holstein.

21. Variable Star. Second quarter nineteenth century. 41″ x 38″. The ingenious placement of interlocking stars creates a subtle geometric design that nearly overpowers the understated central block. Collection of Linda and Irwin Berman.

22. Star of Bethlehem quilt top with appliquéd chintz cutouts and Variable Star border. Second quarter nineteenth century. 48″ x 46″. Glazed polychrome chintz with motifs of exotic birds and flowers was fashionable in this period. This is a rare miniature interpretation of a full-size pattern often executed in very large quilts, sometimes measuring over ten feet in length and width. Collection of George E. Schoellkopf.

24. Four-Patch variation. Second quarter nineteenth century. 45″ x 41″. Here is a variation of the simplest quilt-making pattern—the Four-Patch—significantly altered with elongated points to form Four Pointed Stars. White background triangles form an illusion of circles (or, from another viewpoint, yet another Star variation). A multitude of beautiful period fabrics are used to great advantage in a rich arrangement of warm colors. Photograph courtesy Kelter-Malcé Antiques, New York.

23. Sunburst. c. 1850. Pennsylvania. 48″ x 48″. This radiant explosion of light and color gives the illusion of constant movement originating from a single chintz flower in the center star. Here is a masterful manipulation of visual design with textiles. Photograph courtesy Kelter-Malcé Antiques, New York.

25. Feathered Star. Second quarter nineteenth century. New England. 38″ x 41″. The corners of the central block appear to be tugged at by tiny "flocks" of Geese-in-Flight, a charming detail that adds a bit of tension to this otherwise serene piece. Collection of Linda and Irwin Berman.

26. Star of Bethlehem quilt top, with multiple borders of Sawtooth and Nine-Patch. Second quarter nineteenth century. Pennsylvania. 62″ x 62″. The maker of this impressive showpiece may have enjoyed piecing more than quilting, and so postponed finishing it. Photograph courtesy Bill Gallick and Tony Ellis.

27. *Louisa 1851*. Framed Center quilt. Pieced and appliqué. New York State. 54″ x 43″. Probably made to celebrate the birth of a baby girl, this is a joyous rendition of the Central Medallion motif charmingly framed with Geese-in-Flight alternating with strips of rose-pattern chintz. The simple straight-line quilting was obviously of less interest to the maker than the beguiling appliqué and piecework.

28. Pieced and appliqué crib quilt, Central Medallion framed by Flying Geese and LeMoyne Stars. c. 1850. 41″ x 40″. The Central Medallion style, consisting of a framed center focal point surrounded by multiple borders in a variety of patterns, enjoyed widespread popularity in English and American quilts of the late eighteenth and early nineteenth century. This magnificent crib quilt, one of the finest surviving, features a center block of floral-print appliqué cutouts enclosed by resplendent pieced and appliquéd borders anchored with a star in each of the four corners. All of the sublime details of the most important of nineteenth-century Medallion quilts are here, brilliantly encapsulated in miniature. Collection of Linda and Irwin Berman.

29. Mosaic Star. Mid-nineteenth century. Pennsylvania. 43″ x 43″. Starting with a central six-pointed-star pattern, the quilter quickly switched to random motifs including stars and hearts scattered on a white ground, framed with a Sawtooth border and four corner Stars. Photograph courtesy Mr. and Mrs. Richard Flanders Smith.

30. Printed handkerchief quilt. c. 1865. Maine. 53″ x 50″. Cotton handkerchiefs such as those manufactured by John Hewson were printed in America from the beginning of the eighteenth century onward and were sometimes used as central motifs for quilts, both large and small. Depictions of subjects appealing to children were offered by several textile printers, including sports, birds, animals, songs, verses, stories, and the circus. Collection of Linda and Irwin Berman.

31. Northumberland Star. c. 1865. 44¾″ x 39½″. This design, which includes both piecework and appliqué, requires a highly skilled quiltmaker. A compulsive energy for cutting and piecing is reflected (use a magnifying glass) in the tiny center block, which is meticulously divided on the diagonal and secured in place. Collection of Linda and Irwin Berman.

32. Double Irish Chain. Third quarter nineteenth century. Pennsylvania. 42″ x 41″. A favorite pattern of many quiltmakers, this example is perfectly balanced in both geometry and color. Photograph courtesy Sandra Mitchell.

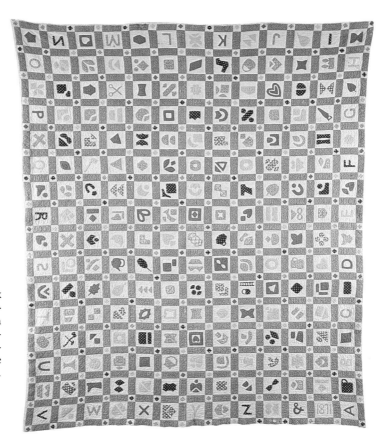

33. Primer quilt. Dated 1871. New York State. 77″ x 62″. Dozens of tiny realistic and abstract images delight—and puzzle—the viewer. A child's education appears to be the theme here, and one feels compelled to play "name the block." The alphabet provides both a decorative border and a good basic lesson. Collection of Mr. and Mrs. Peter M. Brant.

34. Framed Center quilt. Third quarter nineteenth century. 31″ x 31½″. Geese-in-Flight borders frame a calico "wheel" that seems to burst from a sawtooth-edged center square. Warm colors and good quilting add appeal to this animated creation. Photograph courtesy Robert E. Kinnaman and Brian A. Ramaekers. Private collection.

35. Windmill Blades. c. 1875. 46″ x 46″. This magnificent interpretation of a Log Cabin variation appears to make time stand still, seemingly capturing and holding forever in place the rapidly spinning blades. Collection of Linda and Irwin Berman.

36. Pieced and appliquéd quilt top. c. 1875. 44″ x 43″. This appliquéd and pieced pictorial top captures some of the most delightful qualities of folk art with its rather curious perspective, clever use of patterned materials, and familiar subject matter. In modern times artisans such as the maker of this pièce de résistance are greatly missed. Collection of Christophe de Menil.

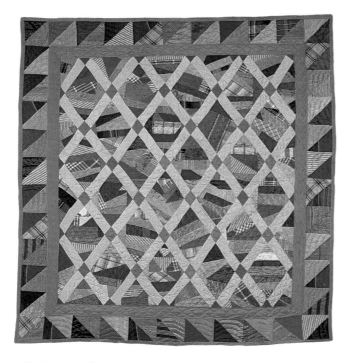

37. Contained crazy quilt. c. 1870. New York State. 41″ x 44″. A beige latticework defines this scintillating assemblage of brilliantly colored silk patches, dramatically punctuated by a hot pink inner border. Photograph courtesy Suzanne Courcier and Robert Wilkins. Private collection.

38. Rocky Glen. Third quarter nineteenth century. New England. 34″ x 27″. A double scalloped border, rarely attempted in quilts of any size, is especially winsome in this diminutive spread. Restraint and remarkable skill enabled the anonymous maker to create a beguiling miniature. Photograph courtesy Robert E. Kinnaman and Brian A. Ramaekers. Private collection.

39. Star of Bethlehem. c. 1880. Pennsylvania. 45″ x 44″. The finely appliquéd tulips and vine border add great verve to this Pennsylvania German delight. Collection of Deborah Wiss.

40. Pieced quilt top. c. 1880. 33″ x 32″. Tiny triangles glide easily in all directions from a central Square-Within-a-Square in this energetic patchwork. Collection of Pie Galinat and Robert Self.

41. Album Patch. c. 1880. Pennsylvania. 41½″ x 38½″. Forty-two blocks of harmoniously colored patches are separated by a pleasant green calico, forming a perfectly balanced small treasure. Photograph courtesy Robert E. Kinnaman and Brian A. Ramaekers. Private collection.

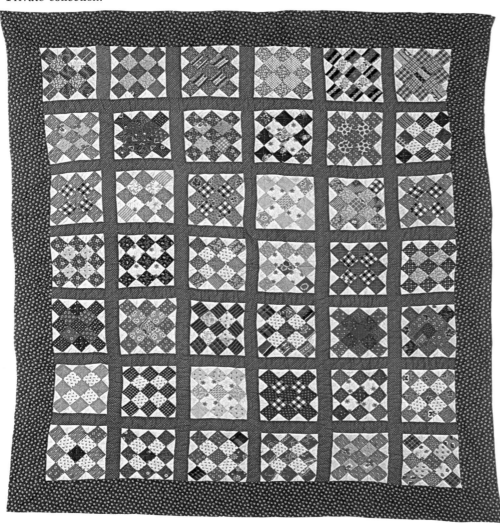

42. Stars. c. 1880. New York State. 42½″ x 37″. Repeated stars in white-dotted blue calico are effectively framed with a grid and swag border of the same material in this beautifully quilted miniature.

43. Sunburst. c. 1885. Lehigh County, Pennsylvania. 39″ x 42″. Thirty-six miniature quilt blocks, separated by a blue cross and surrounded on three sides by rows of Variable Star blocks and on the fourth side with a Birds in Air variation, form the basis for the design. A bit crudely pieced and quilted, but imaginative, this is a mate to an almost identical, well-worn quilt from the same area, probably made by the same maker for two siblings. Collection of Richard and Rosemarie Machmer.

44. Star quilt top. c. 1880. New York State. 42″ x 42″. Eight smaller stars surround a Central Star in this beautifully presented reduction of one of the earliest quilt motifs —the Framed Medallion. Collection of Marcia Delman.

45. Baskets. c. 1880. New York State. 38″ x 32″. Dozens of Basket variations can be found, but few are executed so simply and strikingly as this small abstract, done in peas and carrots colors. Collection of Dr. and Mrs. Ronald Brady.

46. Delectable Mountains. c. 1885. Berks County, Pennsylvania. 36″ x 36″. Probably Mennonite, a characteristic of which is the bright red and yellow solid alternating sawtooth, this pattern is rare in large quilts; in miniature, this is perhaps one of a kind. Collection of Richard and Rosemarie Machmer.

47. Rooster crazy quilt. c. 1885. 39″ x 39½″. The proud embroidered rooster seems startled to find himself standing in the center of this amusing comforter, surrounded by random patches from the quiltmaker's rather humble scrap bag. Collection of Linda and Irwin Berman.

48. Rainbow or Joseph's Coat. c. 1885. Pennsylvania. 64″ x 60″. This simple yet powerful pattern belonging to the Mennonite people of Pennsylvania expresses their fondness for vivid color and bold design. Collection of Phyllis Haders.

49. Star Medallion quilt top. c. 1885. Probably Mennonite. Pennsylvania. 31″ x 31″. Bright hues splash brilliantly within colorfully fluctuating borders. Photograph courtesy Judy Corman.

50. Log Cabin–Barn Raising variation. c. 1880. Pennsylvania. 46″ x 46″. One of the most popular patterns for over a century, this variation is said to represent a bird's-eye view of a log cabin structure ready for raising. Collection of David Pottinger.

51. T. c. 1885. 45″ x 50″. This design is exactly twenty-five percent of the Monkey Wrench pattern, delightfully sewn in a cheerful variety of colorful prints. Collection of Nancy and Gary Stass.

52. Baskets. c. 1885. New York State. 44″ x 44″. Order and neatness permeate this meticulous, skillfully worked piece, employing a spare design together with machinelike accuracy to create an admirable balance. Collection of Elizabeth Weisman.

53. Delectable Mountains. c. 1885. New Jersey. 56″ x 38″. The long narrow proportions of this unusually handsome quilt were dictated by the choice of two center squares, enhanced by red and green zigzag borders. Collection of Linda and Irwin Berman.

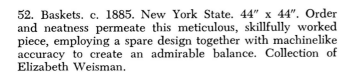

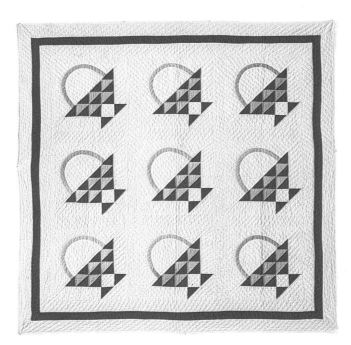

54. Birds in Air variation. c. 1885. Pennsylvania. 60″ x 40″. This graphic Pennsylvania German piecework is a rhythmic composition of bright red and yellow calico blocks intersecting V-shaped formations of birds in flight in a lively abstract design. Elements of Wild Goose Chase and Ocean Waves inspired this brisk geometric. Photograph courtesy M. Finkel and Daughter.

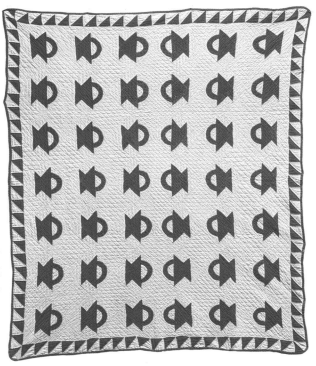

55. Baskets. c. 1885. New York State. 37″ x 31″. The basket motif, with its great personal appeal, appeared early in quiltmaking and was interpreted in dozens of styles. The curved handles here are a zestful foil for the sharp angles of the bases and Sawtooth border. Collection of Elizabeth Weisman.

56. Pieced quilt top. c. 1895. 51½" x 35". The overlay of lines, using one color on white and framed by a strict linear border within the reinforcing confines of set dimensions, creates an interesting optical effect. Collection of Paul and Muffin Cunnion.

57. Philadelphia Pavement variation. c. 1895. Pennsylvania. 41" x 41". This pattern is said to be a stylistic representation of the cobblestone streets of old Philadelphia. Hundreds of tiny calico pieces are artfully grouped to form a sensational geometric "textile painting." Collection of Linda and Irwin Berman.

58. Schoolhouse. c. 1925. Midwest. 36″ x 24″. The one-room schoolhouse, a favorite historical source of inspiration for quilters, is the basis for a dynamic, geometric, and imaginative design. Photograph courtesy Timothy and Pamela Hill.

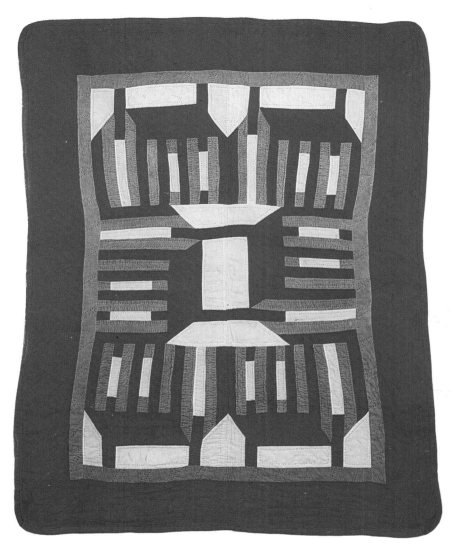

59. Rainbow. Early twentieth century. Pennsylvania. 54″ x 35″. This somewhat primitive version of a gloriously simple pattern was probably made by the young daughter of a Mennonite quiltmaker attempting to imitate on a small scale the stately beauty of a full-size Joseph's Coat. Collection of Gail van der Hoof and Jonathan Holstein.

60. Circus. 47″ x 61″. 1910. Gilmer, Texas. Hand-pieced and quilted by Myrtle Augusta Patterson for her son Clovis Calvin Patterson. An unusual effect is achieved in this pictorial quilt by the use of piecework, a rare method in this case where many quilters would have chosen to use appliqué. Although the motifs were probably inspired by a commercial pattern, the success of the quilt is no less charming because of the color choice, arrangements of the blocks, and an overall whimsical effect. Collection of Karey Patterson Bresenhan.

61. Rising Sun. c. 1915. Pennsylvania. 40″ x 40″. This is just one of over a half dozen similar Star quilts made by one Pennsylvania quiltmaker in various sizes from small to full-size, presumably for each member of the family. Some Pennsylvanians call this Rising Sun because the little stars surrounding the central Star of Bethlehem are seen disappearing as the sun rises. Collection of Donald Leiby.

62. Irish Chain variation. c. 1920. Found in Ohio. 41″ x 36″. The double inner frame is reminiscent of Amish quilts but the simple scalloped border is a twentieth-century decorative addition. The quilt exhibits strength of design with a somewhat delicate effect. Private collection.

63. Lone Star. c. 1925. Found in Washington, D.C. 34″ x 34″. Fine quilting, precise piecework, and first-rate color selection enrich this twentieth-century example of one of the most popular traditional quilt patterns. Collection of Esprit de Corps.

65. *Athens Farewell*. 1979. Ohio. 60″ x 54″. This daring contemporary piece by Nancy Crow offers evidence that the inventive spirit of past quiltmaking has not entirely disappeared. The Fanny's Fans in the corner blocks are traditional, but the rest of the fascinating composition is truly unconventional—a rollicking, rhythmic abstraction by a boldly expressive artist. Collection of the artist.

64. Alphabet. c. 1930. Pennsylvania. 46″ x 32″. An appealing introduction to the ABCs is presented in this ingratiating "teaching aid." Collection of Gail van der Hoof and Jonathan Holstein.

APPLIQUÉ QUILTS

66. Appliqué chintz cutout. c. 1835. 42½″ x 38½″. This quilt has such style and elegance it must have been used just for Sunday best. Collection of Mr. and Mrs. Foster McCarl, Jr.

67. Basket of Flowers appliqué. Early nineteenth century. Found in New England. 41″ x 40″. The delicacy and restraint of this piece are admirable, with cutout flowers appliquéd on a plain, finely quilted ground. The stenciled inner frame is extremely rare in quilts of any size. Collection of Linda and Irwin Berman.

68. Appliqué quilt. First half nineteenth century. 36″ x 36″. Stuffed grapes and appliquéd leaves encircle a finely quilted ground, framed with a lace and tassel border, to form a rare example of superb needlework. Photograph courtesy Robert E. Kinnaman and Brian A. Ramaekers. Private collection.

69. Appliqué quilt top. First half nineteenth century. New England. 46″ x 36″. Exquisite brown prints cut into leaf forms are attached to a plain ground in a deliberately restrained palette. Photograph courtesy Robert E. Kinnaman and Brian A. Ramaekers. Private collection.

70. Chintz cutout appliqué. Second quarter nineteenth century. Found in New York State. 34″ x 30″. A finely quilted white background serves as a canvas for exotic "painted" birds surrounding an elegant urn of flowers in this special piece, which is definitely not for everyday use. Photograph courtesy Barry Cohen. Collection of Linda and Irwin Berman.

71. Eagle appliqué. c. 1850. Copake, New York. Signed Rachie T. Strever. 34″ x 34″. Encircling the fine red eagle are thirteen stars—eight appliquéd and five quilted—representing the thirteen original Colonies, plus a glorious wreath of flowers, leaves, and seven delightfully primitive birds.

72. Album quilt. Mid-nineteenth century. Chester County, Pennsylvania. 54" x 43½". Album quilts consist of differently patterned blocks, sometimes made by several family members or friends for a loved one. The uniformity of workmanship in such pieces as this indicates that the work was made by one person as a showcase of her versatility in pattern design. Collection of Nancy and Gary Stass.

73. Album quilt. Mid-nineteenth century. Pennsylvania. 38" x 34½". The generous stuffing of each motif with wads of cotton achieves an impressive three-dimensional effect in this jubilant example. Currently owned by a descendant of the maker, this is truly an enchanting heirloom, complete with what seem to be some very "happy-faced" flowers. Private collection.

74. Baltimore album quilt. c. 1862. Patuxent, Maryland. 40″ x 40″. Baltimore quilters produced some of the most extraordinary appliquéd spreads ever made. One theory is that there were even professional quilters from whom one could purchase individual, exquisitely hand-stitched blocks to enhance one's own quilt. This remarkable piece was done entirely by Mrs. Noah I. Donaldson, an ancestor of its present owner, for her fifth child. Photograph courtesy Myron Miller. Private collection.

75. Heart and Hat. Mid-nineteenth century. Yonkers, New York. 34½″ x 32½″. This romantic miniature, a textile valentine in crib quilt form, is inscribed: "A heart I send, Young Squire Baldwin/Reject it not I do implore thee/A warm reception may it meet/My name a Secret I must keep./Old Maid." How the story ended remains a tantalizing secret. Collection of Linda and Irwin Berman.

76. Pots of Flowers appliqué. Mid-nineteenth century. New England. 31″ x 30″. The small-scale and tightly executed design add delight to this unique variation. Photograph courtesy Robert E. Kinnaman and Brian A. Ramaekers.

77. Eagle appliqué quilt top. c. 1855. Pennsylvania. 35″ x 35″. This ebullient eagle appears literally to be jumping for joy in a shower of stars, and the pots of flowers happily follow suit.

78. Double Hearts appliqué. c. 1860. Pennsylvania. 41½″ x 41½″. Hearts have long been a favorite motif in American folk art, especially with the Pennsylvania Germans. The captivating border, consisting of a fence of hearts, effectively contains an irresistible center arrangement of the traditional romantic symbol. Collection of George E. Schoellkopf.

79. Buds and Swags appliqué. 1850–1860. Pennsylvania. 34″ x 33″. Green swags with red tassels and stars make a sprightly frame for the rosebuds that surround "Emma." The quilt probably celebrates the birth of a daughter. Collection of Caroline Baker.

80. Wreath appliqué. 1850–1860. 42½″ x 34″. The most exciting quilts, small or large, are those made in original designs by those who used their knowledge of familiar patterns and traditional techniques to create a bold, new, totally individual composition. Private collection.

81. Tulip Cross. c. 1865. Pennsylvania. 42″ x 42″. This cheerful Pennsylvania German floral with swag border expertly fills the space of the quilt, and quilted leaves echo the pattern and enhance the texture. Collection of Richard and Rosemarie Machmer.

82. John M. Lyon Centennial Christmas quilt. 1876. New York State. 41½″ x 41½″. What better way to celebrate the Christmas of America's Centennial year than to have stitched this beautiful textile? The difficult reverse-appliqué technique is used here, in which the designs are cut out from the background and then filled with colored fabrics. Collection of Linda and Irwin Berman.

83. Appliqué quilt. Third quarter nineteenth century. Pennsylvania. 42″ x 37½″. The abstract devices here are an interesting assortment of primitive designs, several of which were cut out of fabrics much as one cuts out paper snowflakes. Private collection.

84. Rose Cross appliqué. c. 1880. Pennsylvania. 38″ x 39″. A complex combination of piecework and appliqué, this outstanding quilt splendidly represents the best of nineteenth-century Pennsylvania German work. Collection of Linda and Irwin Berman.

85. Cock's Comb appliqué. c. 1890. Pennsylvania, probably Mennonite. 44″ x 44″. Flat planes of color form a symmetrical floral design in this Pennsylvania German prize. Collection of Mr. and Mrs. Eugene Zuriff.

86. Sawtooth Diamond with floral appliqué. c. 1890. Made by Edna E. Myer of Cleona, Lebanon County, Pennsylvania. 49″ x 49″. A striking Sawtooth Diamond and dramatic floral silhouettes join in this vibrant design, expertly punctuated with four bright stars. Collection of Dr. and Mrs. Donald Herr.

87. Appliqué. c. 1890. Pennsylvania, probably Mennonite. 43″ x 45″. Pennsylvania quiltmakers were very fond of the color pumpkin orange and often used it as an eye-catching background for a forceful graphic abstract design such as this one-of-a-kind quilt. Collection of Stella Rubin.

88. Poppy appliqué. c. 1890. Pennsylvania, probably Mennonite. 46″ x 46″. The green calico joining the four blossoms is the only print in this floral of bold solid colors that are characteristic of fine Mennonite quiltmaking. Collection of Richard and Rosemarie Machmer.

89. Pot of Flowers appliqué. Last quarter nineteenth century. 24″ x 18″. This extraordinary primitive is a first-rate example of inspired folk art in textiles. The uneven, off-center central block contains a single, humble flower surrounded by crazy patches and framed with a triumphant vine of leaves. Embroidery adds a touch of hoped-for elegance, which results instead in an irresistible down-home effect. Collection of Timothy and Pamela Hill.

90. Princess Feather appliqué. c. 1880. Pennsylvania. 39″ x 37″. Proud red plumes emblazoned on a pure white ground create a spectacular swirling wheel, abundantly framed with a finely quilted grapevine border. Collection of Elizabeth Weisman.

91. Floral appliqué. c. 1880. Pennsylvania. 44″ x 44″. Simple, graceful blooms are neatly appliquéd in a Sawtooth frame, surrounded by a superbly quilted Running Feather and four additional blossoms decorating each corner. Collection of Elizabeth Weisman.

92. Maple Leaf appliqué. c. 1915. New York State. 42″ x 31″. This original design, found in upstate New York, may have been inspired by Canadian friends or relatives. Each slightly different leaf appears to have fallen into a red frame and been captured there for our lasting enjoyment. Collection of Caroline Baker.

93. Starburst variation. c. 1915. Maine. 37″ x 30″. Quilt patterns such as this energetic example offer delight and amusement and demonstrate the ageless appeal of originality.

94. Cross appliqué with swag border. Early twentieth century. Maine. 43″ x 37″. Religious themes provided inspiration for some quiltmakers, but few got into the spirit with such exuberance as this jubilant tribute to "Jesus Baby." Photograph courtesy Kelter-Malcé Antiques, New York.

95. Hawaiian appliqué. Hawaiian Islands. 30″ x 30″. The abstract design, appliquéd c. 1900 and quilted more recently, is a rare miniature example of the Hawaiian method of cutting patterns in large overall motifs. Their meaning often remained the secret of the makers. Collection of Phyllis Haders.

96. Pictorial appliqué. c. 1930. Pennsylvania. 35″ x 48″. A marionette show is colorfully depicted in this confection, which shows "redheads" both running and watching the performance. Photograph courtesy Hovey and Evelyn Gleason. Private collection.

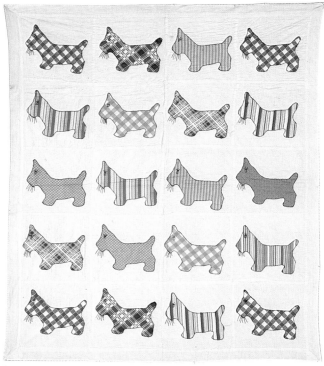

97. Storybook appliqué. c. 1930. Minnesota. 62″ x 41″. Commercial kits can offer valuable assistance to quilters, although the results are seldom as charming and successful as this example from the period 1930–1940.

98. Terriers appliqué. c. 1930. Pennsylvania. 47″ x 40″. Gingham and striped pups form a delightful forerunner of Pop art, but they are infinitely more warmly appealing. Collection of Barbara Bersell.

99. Autumn Leaves appliqué. c. 1940. Pennsylvania. 68″ x 63″. Vines with multicolored leaves encircle a lovely and fanciful arrangement in this whimsical framed-center quilt. Private collection.

AMISH QUILTS

100. Grandmother's Dream. 1890–1910. Lancaster County, Pennsylvania. 44″ x 44″. Combined here are two of the three traditional Pennsylvania Amish quilt patterns: the Diamond, which may have been inspired by designs from old Amish hymnal covers; and Sunshine and Shadow, with its striking arrangements of light and dark patches. The quilting patterns are scaled-down versions of the full-size Pennsylvania Amish quilts and contribute significantly to this remarkable miniature. Collection of Dr. and Mrs. Donald Herr.

101. Spiderweb Star. Early twentieth century. Ohio Amish. 40″ x 34″. This pattern was rarely used in Amish quilts and is even more unusual in its use of the off-white inner frame and three pinwheels that punctuate this very unconventional piece. Collection of Darwin Bearley.

102. Monkey Wrench. Early twentieth century. Ohio Amish. 42″ x 33″. A common pattern outside Amish communities, this version is rendered unmistakably Amish by the distinctive palette. Collection of Darwin Bearley.

103. One-Patch variation. Early twentieth century. Ohio Amish. 47″ x 38″. The rich earthy hues and mellow patina are the outstanding features of this deceptively simple and charming quilt. The Amish quilters manipulate simple colors in unusual combinations, achieving an overall effect of contained vitality.

104. Streak O'Lightning. Early twentieth century. Ohio Amish. 37½" x 28¼". This arresting pattern takes on a new dimension when executed in these unusual colors. Private collection.

105. Baskets. c. 1910. Shipshewana, Indiana. 39" x 33". The juxtaposition of pattern and color in this irresistible piece offers a soothing calm to the viewer, suggesting the quiet inner strength of the maker. Collection of David Pottinger.

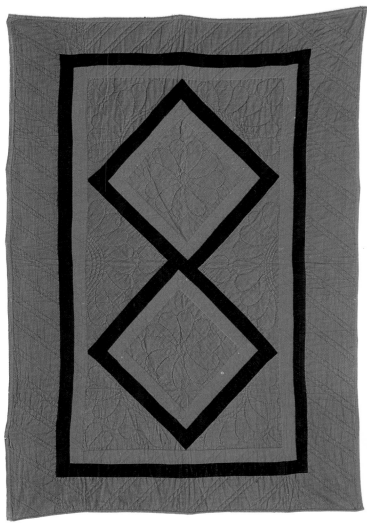

106. Double Diamond. c. 1920. 42½″ x 29″. Indiana. Unique use of Amish Diamond in a square, enriched by lush quilting filling the spaces around the design, interspersed with several hearts. The dramatic contrast of red and black is somewhat softened by the brown ground. Photograph courtesy David Pottinger.

107. Double X variation. c. 1920. Ohio Amish. 42″ x 33″. An illusion of translucence—a stained-glass effect—is achieved by the use of glowing colors and the shimmering finish of the polished cotton. Private collection.

108. Carolina Lily. c. 1920. Ohio Amish. 47″ x 32″. The serene beauty of this quilt reflects the simple Amish way of life and its power lies in its unadorned integrity, which is almost spiritual in its effect. This is a superb example of an Amish interpretation of an old nineteenth-century quilt pattern from outside the community, the only one known using this motif. Collection of Linda and Irwin Berman.

109. Bear's Paw. c. 1920. Indiana Amish. 33″ x 35″. Also called Duck's-Foot-in-the-Mud, here is a delightful Amish adaptation of an old motif. The black background was much used by midwestern Amish quiltmakers in the 1920s and 1930s. Collection of David Pottinger.

110. One-Patch. c. 1920. Ohio. 34″ x 30″. Presented here in simple form is a good sampling of the Amish palette, demonstrating the power of stark simplicity. Collection of Phyllis Haders.

111. Old Maid's Puzzle. c. 1925. Ohio Amish. 41″ x 32″. Through the arrangement of blocks and colors a fascinating geometric design emerges, with the eye discovering several patterns within the pattern. Although this design consists of only six blocks, the way in which they have been turned to meet each other causes several geometric formations to occur. Two blocks of completely different patterns emerge in the center: one a Square-Within-a-Square, the other a Shoofly, surrounded by fragments of Variable Star. This inventive quilt is a fine example of the quiltmaker's control of her medium and is a delightfully original design. Photograph courtesy Robert E. Kinnaman and Brian A. Ramaekers. Private collection.

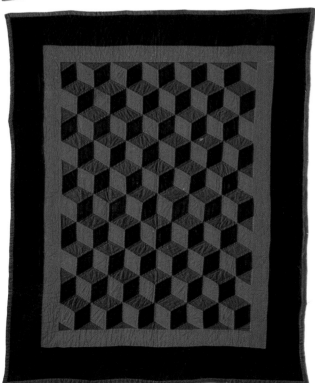

112. Tumbling Blocks. c. 1925. Ohio Amish. 48″ x 38″. This classic design motif, also called Stair Steps, dates back to ancient times and is particularly successful here, executed with machinelike accuracy and perfectly balanced contrasting colors. Private collection.

113. Corn and Beans. c. 1925. Ohio Amish. 41″ x 30″. This playful divertissement is handsomely complex. Collection of Linda and Irwin Berman.

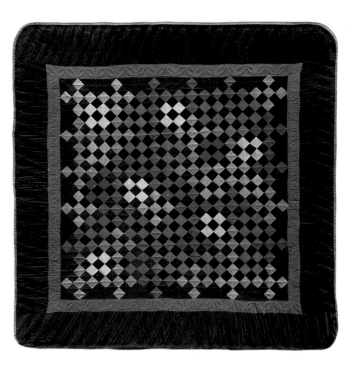

114. Log Cabin–Light and Dark variation. c. 1925. Ohio Amish. 31″ x 27″. The usual Light and Dark variation is known for its sharply contrasting colors; however, this Amish miniature contains more subtle tonal variations in richly colored wools, resulting in a completely different effect. Two of the corner blocks are reversed for added interest. Collection of Darwin Bearley.

115. Nine-Patch. c. 1925. Ohio. 40″ x 42″. Here, again, a simple pattern is made effective by the seemingly random placement of color resulting in a nicely balanced overall effect, warmly framed with a coral inner border. Photograph courtesy Robert E. Kinnaman and Brian A. Ramaekers. Private collection.

116. Log Cabin–Straight Furrows variation. c. 1925. Ohio. 38″ x 31″. The solid earth colors chosen by the maker of this splendid piece remind us of the fundamentally plain, unassuming habits of a devoted religious sect rooted in a sober outlook on life. Collection of Darwin Bearley.

117. Plain Quilt. c. 1925. Holmes County, Ohio. 41″ x 41″. Here is the essence of superior Ohio Amish quiltmaking. The two inner frames of blue on a black ground produce a scintillating and dramatic effect. The quilting, uninterrupted by complex piecework, is of the highest quality and reminiscent of the finest of earlier Amish quilts from Pennsylvania. Collection of Linda and Irwin Berman.

118. Nine-Patch. c. 1925. Ohio or Indiana. 51″ x 40″. Using one of the simplest quilt patterns, an effective composition is achieved by adroit manipulation of color. Collection of David Pottinger.

119. Baskets variation (Cakestand). 1925–1935. Indiana. 54″ x 46″. The straightforward charm of careful color arrangement and understatement of design combine with excellent needlework to form this highly effective quilt. Photograph courtesy David Pottinger. Collection of Rebecca Haarer.

120. Philadelphia Pavement. c. 1930. Iowa Amish. 60″ x 42″. The light colors indicate that this quilt is from a more western Amish settlement. As the Amish traveled westward, their quilts drew more freely on outside influences for patterns and materials. Collection of Walter Bachner.

121. One-Patch. c. 1925. Ohio. 47″ x 38″. A vibrant "checkerboard" emerges from forceful hues of red and blue locked in perpetual tension, giving the viewer's eye a pleasant jolt. Collection of Linda and Irwin Berman.

122. Four-Patch variation. c. 1940. Ohio Amish. 48″ x 39″. A fascinating geometric arrangement of the most elementary of patterns emboldened by a use of color that achieves a mysterious interior illumination. Photograph courtesy Kiracofe and Kile.

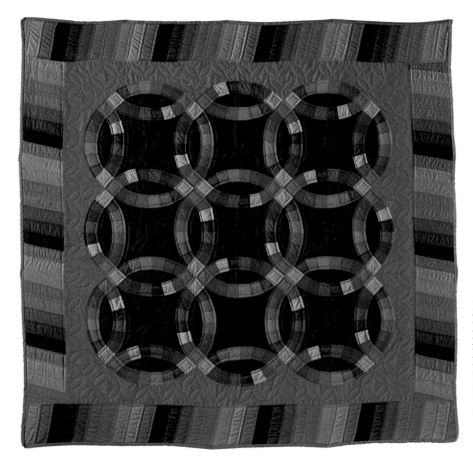

123. Double Wedding Ring. 1978. Indiana. 55½″ x 54½″. A contemporary interpretation of one of the most popular of twentieth-century patterns. The dynamic, intense hues of Amish quilts add a spellbinding dimension not usually found in this familiar design. Photograph courtesy Plain Sewing, Fay Walters.

124. Appliqué picture: *The Nativity*. Early nineteenth century. Descended in the Warner Family of New York and Connecticut. 33½" x 33½". The embroidered inscription reads: *Glory to God in the Highest Peace on Earth and good will to Men Hallelujah*. The Georgian-style architecture depicted in this celebration adds unexpected delight to a joyful interpretation. Photograph courtesy The Henry Francis du Pont Winterthur Museum, Winterthur, Delaware.

125. Pieced and appliqué picture of an English half-timber house. London, England. c. 1865. 25" x 31". Pictures made with pieced or appliqué techniques are quite rare. This fascinating example from England, a mosaic composed of three-quarter-inch silk squares, is included for the sake of comparison with American work of the same period. Photograph courtesy Cora Ginsburg.

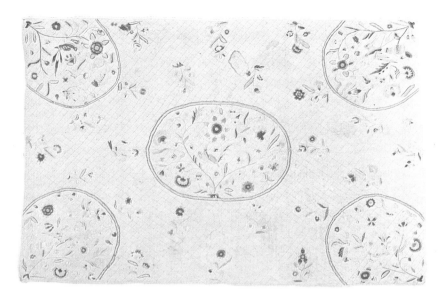

126. Christening blanket. Mid-eighteenth century. Possibly Connecticut. 23″ x 34½″. Crewel-embroidered christening blankets, precursors of nineteenth-century American crib quilts, were found in affluent Colonial households. Old Sturbridge Village, Sturbridge, Massachusetts.

127. Table cover. Early nineteenth century. New Hampshire. 31″ x 33″. This wonderful crewel-embroidered piece, enhanced with appliquéd pots of flowers, was found under a sleeping cat in a barn. Collection of Gail van der Hoof and Jonathan Holstein.

128. Table cover with appliqué hearts and flowers. First quarter nineteenth century. 21″ x 28½″. A strong command of layered appliqué techniques is evident in this rare cover of wool, cotton, linen, and silk. Collection of Grace and Elliot Snyder.

129. & 130. Pair of table covers. First half nineteenth century. Probably New Bedford, Massachusetts. 27½″ x 29¾″ and 20½″ x 26″. Flowers growing in perfect symmetry and a fanciful Tree of Life are appliquéd in wool on a linen ground. Collection of Grace and Elliot Snyder.

71

131. Table cover. 1830–1840. New England. 30″ x 68″. Wool appliqué carnations and wildflowers in pots were popular motifs for elegant quilts, some of which were inspired by late eighteenth- and early nineteenth-century bed rug motifs. Collection of Grace and Elliot Snyder.

132. Appliqué table cover. Second quarter nineteenth century. New York State. 33″ x 31″. Superb appliqué work and a sublime sense of design and color have created a "painting" in this theoremlike cotton cover. Collection of Joy and Jack Piscopo.

133. Table cover. 1820–1840. 28½″ x 50″. Appliqué, wool with cotton and yarn sewn details. This appliqué painting, found in Otisfield, Maine, depicts the actual house containing the attic in which it was found. Collection of Stephen and Eleanor Score.

134. Table cover. Signed and dated 1864. Made by Persius Bradbury of Norway, Maine. 27″ x 43″. This wool appliqué cover was made in the style of an album quilt.

135. Cushion cover with boxing. 1780–1800. Groton, Connecticut. Cushion 14½″ x 17″, Boxing 3¾″ x 19½″. These appliquéd and embroidered textiles were obtained directly from descendants of the Chapman family of Groton, who removed them from stuffed cushions in a great-grandfather's banister-back chair. Photograph courtesy Dena S. Katzenberg, The Baltimore Museum of Art, Baltimore, Maryland.

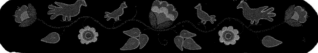

136. Appliqué rug with braided border. Third quarter nineteenth century. 28″ x 43″. Above the inscription *We's Free* two tiny figures dance among a peaceable grouping of wool appliqué animals and a little girl dressed in a pink dress of soft leather, probably a remnant of a kid glove. Private collection.

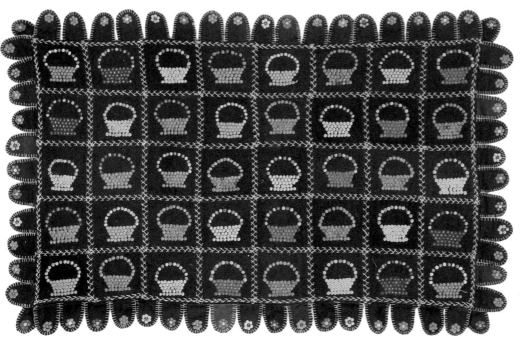

137. Penny-rug table cover. Second half nineteenth century. New England. 27″ x 41″. Bits of "pennies" of felt form colorful Baskets, a favorite patchwork quilt pattern. Photograph courtesy Jacqueline and John Sideli.

138. Crochet appliqué on home-spun. Late nineteenth century. Found in Tennessee. 32″ x 28½″. Animals and people surround a Tree of Life in an original interpretation of motifs found in pictorial quilts.

139. Appliqué pillow sham (one of a pair). Signed and dated *Anna (R.?) Lane 1864*. Pennsylvania. 37″ x 17″. Fine appliqué stitching and a carefully planned design create a pair of graceful accessories for a mid-nineteenth-century appliqué quilt. Collection of Sally Clark.

140. Hearts and Tulips pillow sham. Third quarter nineteenth century. 22½" x 15". The charming motifs of hearts and tulips indicate a Pennsylvania origin. The sham probably embellished the outside of a pillow during the daytime in a rural household. Collection of Nancy and Gary Stass.

141. Variable Star pillow sham (one of a pair). 1865–1875. Pennsylvania. 29" x 17". Bright colors and bold designs were characteristic of Pennsylvania German quiltmakers. Collection of Dr. and Mrs. Donald Herr.

142. Pillow sham (front and back, one of a pair). Pieced stars. c. 1880. Pennsylvania. 26" x 17". Elaborate quilting and exact piecework combine to form this striking example. Finely quilted pillow shams made in England in the late seventeenth through the eighteenth centuries served as models for those made in late nineteenth-century America. Collection of Dr. and Mrs. Donald Herr.

143. Nine-Patch variation pieced pillow sham. c. 1890. Pennsylvania. 30″ x 19″. The lively patchwork of late nineteenth-century Pennsylvania is irresistible. Collection of Mr. and Mrs. Peter Findlay.

144. Yo-yo Basket of Flowers pillow sham. c. 1930. Iowa. 17″ x 16″. This amusing confection consists of tiny gathered circles sewn on a black ground with appliquéd stems and leaves. The "yo-yos" are one-half the size usually found in typical examples. Collection of Mr. and Mrs. Sherman Saperstein.

145. Hit and Miss variation doll quilt. Third quarter nineteenth century. 15½″ x 19½″ including 4″ drop. Delicate silk patches were pieced into a lovely spread, which fits easily on a miniature four-poster bed, with two corners left open for that purpose. Collection of Betty Sterling.

146. Postage Stamp doll quilt. c. 1875. New England. 15″ x 13″. A pleasant color arrangement adds appeal to this miniature. Photograph courtesy André Gürtler.

147. Cross variation. c. 1875. Pennsylvania. 26½″ x 20″. This charming patchwork design is animated yet firmly anchored in place. There are two possible slip-ups, one of which may have been the "Devil's eye," a deliberate flaw to show humility. The other shows that to err is human. Collection of Robert E. Kinnaman and Brian A. Ramaekers.

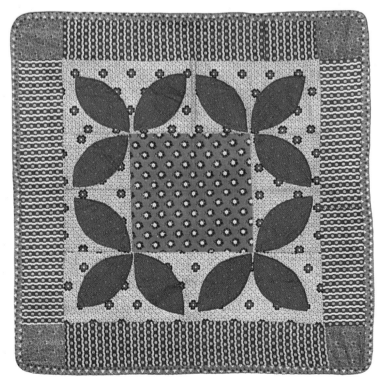

148. Honey Bee. c. 1875. Pennsylvania. 17″ x 17″. The tabs on two corners indicate the possibility that this small patchwork was made to decorate a wall. Collection of Gail van der Hoof and Jonathan Holstein.

149. Patriotic doll quilt. c. 1876. 15″ x 12½″. Printed fragment of flag material. Any child's doll would feel a surge of patriotism at the sight of this amusing "make-do." Photograph courtesy Gloria List. Collection of Kiracofe and Kile.

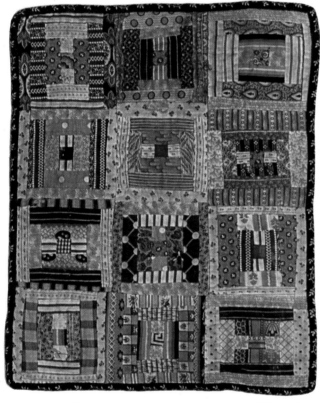

150. Log Cabin–Courthouse Steps variation doll quilt. c. 1880. Pennsylvania. 12″ x 9″. Arranged here are tiny "logs" of beautiful late nineteenth-century calicoes in soothing browns and blues. Collection of Molly Epstein.

151. Melon Patch doll quilt. c. 1880. 23″ x 16″. This allover pattern is difficult in full scale; working the curved lines in miniature required considerable patience. Collection of Nancy and Gary Stass.

152. Hearts doll quilt. c. 1880. 18¼" x 17". A miniature pop art doll quilt such as this is irresistible. Collection of Nancy and Gary Stass.

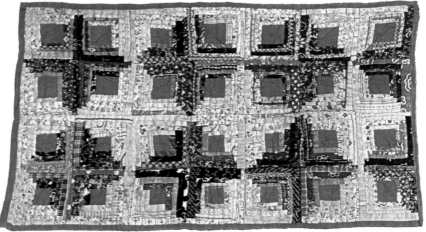

153. Log Cabin–Light and Dark variation doll quilt. c. 1885. Pennsylvania. 8½" x 14". A sensational miniature was created here by skillful sewing of tiny "logs," tightly arranged in a difficult variation of this popular pattern. Photograph courtesy Gloria List. Collection of Kiracofe and Kile.

154. Log Cabin–Courthouse Steps variation doll quilt. c. 1885. Pennsylvania. 19" x 19". Collection of Gail van der Hoof and Jonathan Holstein.

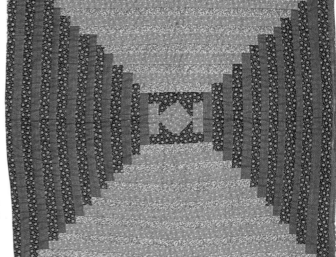

155. Log Cabin doll quilt. c. 1890. 26½″ x 23″. Satin with braided edge. Bright red and icy white, punctuated with tiny, blue center squares, shimmer in an exuberant interpretation of a traditional pattern. Photograph courtesy Gloria List. Collection of Kiracofe and Kile.

156. Crazy doll quilt. c. 1900. 17″ x 11″. This abstract cotton quilt may have been a practice piece made by a child. Private collection.

157. Appliqué picture. Early twentieth century. Pennsylvania. 22″ x 17″. This charming country scene was probably created with an appliqué kit from a specialty store. Collection of Elizabeth Weisman.

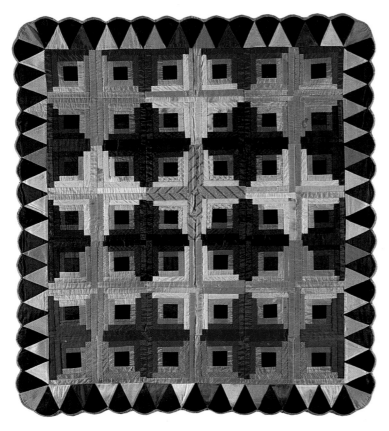

158. Log Cabin–Light and Dark. Last quarter nineteenth century. New England. 38″ x 32″. A scalloped border frames a stained-glass-window effect using unusually soft colors for the late Victorian style. Photograph courtesy Robert E. Kinnaman and Brian A. Ramaekers. Private collection.

159. Victorian Sunburst. c. 1885. New England. 48″ x 48″. Miniature oil paintings and printed textile pictures adorn this satiny showpiece. Private collection.

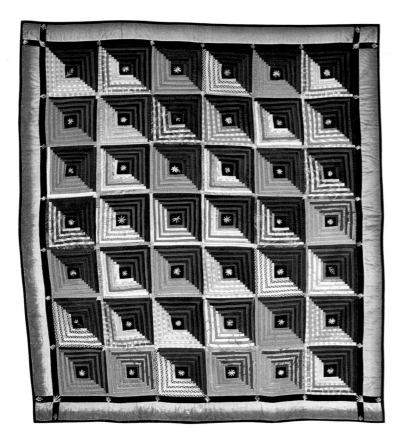

160. Log Cabin. c. 1885. Massachusetts. 51″ x 45″. Silk, satin, and velvet quilts were common in the late nineteenth century, but few were done with the restraint or originality of this silk quilt. Subtle details, such as the embroidered pine needles, and, on the frame, the two adjacent light borders opposite two dark edges—mirroring the individual quilt blocks—are rare. Private collection.

161. Cigar band table cover. 1880–1890. 35″ x 35″. Silk cigar bands and tobacco pouch labels, a popular novelty for late nineteenth-century quiltmakers, are colorfully arranged in this patriotic display. Collection of Raymond Saroff.

162. Cross. c. 1890. 38″ x 33½″. A fascinating stained-glass-window look is achieved through the use of richly colored silks, carefully arranged in a brilliant Four-Patch pattern, with bright diagonal strips giving the effect of a golden overlay. Photograph courtesy David Pottinger. Collection of Rebecca Haarer.

163. Pieced quilt. c. 1890. New Hampshire. 56″ x 51″. Few late Victorian quilts, fashionably rendered in colorful silks, achieved the glittering impact of this outstanding example. Private collection.

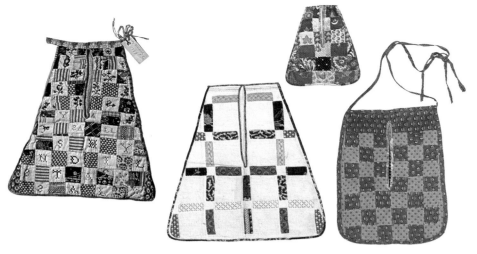

164. Waistpockets. First quarter of nineteenth century. New England, New York State, and Pennsylvania. L. of two largest pieces: 14″. Patchwork waistpockets were handy for carrying sewing supplies and provided still another practical and decorative use for recycled scraps of cotton and wool. One delightful example features scrambled cross-stitched letters spelling *Sally Standish* and is dated *1799.* Collections of Rosemarie Machmer, Kathy Schoemer, and private collection.

165. Sewing cases. Late eighteenth and early nineteenth centuries. New England. L. of largest example: 27″. Needles and thread and other small articles were often stored in fold-up pouches made of decorative patchwork. Collections of H. John and Joan L. Thayer, Old Sturbridge Village, Sturbridge, Massachusetts, and Kelter-Malcé Antiques, New York.

166. Patchwork whimsies. Second half of nineteenth century. Pennsylvania. There may be smaller wonders than these pieced baubles that measure about 3″ wide, but none is more appealing. Can anyone resist a patchwork ball wrapped with tiny patches, each less than one-half inch square, that rattles when given a good shake? As delightful is the curious patchwork pincushion, which appears to be made of a dozen polychrome sausage links. Actually, tiny patches were folded on the diagonal, stuffed, and sewn together with hidden stitches. The final irresistible example of miniature patchwork is the Square-Within-a-Square pillow. Of the many qualifications essential for the quilter, one of the most treasured of all is a ready sense of humor. Collection of Rosemarie Machmer.

PATTERNS AND INSTRUCTIONS
FOR
MAKING YOUR OWN CRIB QUILTS

PATTERNS AND INSTRUCTIONS
FOR
MAKING YOUR OWN CRIB QUILTS

INTRODUCTION

Strong opinions on how to make a crib quilt have been expressed for many years. Readers of *The House Book*,[65] published in 1840, were instructed to use two discarded silk dresses to make a "light and convenient article" for a child's crib, especially useful in a "sick-room" as a morale booster. For reasons unexplained by the author, the quilt was meant to be quilted only in large diamonds, and in another passage, patchwork quilts of old calicoes were declared unfit for use anywhere except in "inferior chambers," where they would work well for the servants' beds. Far more stylish were quilts made entirely of one dark calico or chintz pieced together in long strips, with perhaps a fringe of cotton for true elegance.

Almost one hundred years later an American pattern company pronounced in a 1937 brochure that ". . . children's quilts should definitely be children's quilts and not pale adaptations of grown-up patterns." [66] They provided patterns resembling children's coloring-book figures, with a preponderance of little bunnies.

The patterns offered here illustrate some of the handsome designs from the past. These patterns should be considered only as a starting point—a blueprint for imaginative expression—and not as an inhibiting set of rigid instructions. Individual variations in color and design are welcome, for they make the finished piece unique. While a personally devised pattern that is totally original can be the best of all, these traditional patterns, imaginatively and skillfully executed, are equally to be treasured.

For detailed information on techniques of needlework, such as making templates, mitering corners, or quilting in complex patterns, one should refer to quilting manuals, available in bookstores, libraries, and specialty stores (see list, p. 91); or one can enroll in a quilting class.

Fine stitchery in the quilting enhances the overall appearance of a spread. Machine quilting and tying or "tufting" are shortcuts that seriously detract. If individual skills are not equal to the task of hand quilting, there are church groups and senior citizens associations that still meet regularly at quilting bees and can finish a quilt in a highly competent manner.

Simple, effective quilting patterns, such as parallel lines, can be drawn with a ruler. If they are crossed diagonally, diamonds will be formed throughout. Contour quilting—quilting in concentric lines around the appliquéd designs, following the outlines of the designs—results in an enchanting rhythmic texture throughout the piece, a quilting technique typical of Hawaiian quilts. Illustrated here are a few other favorite quilting patterns, which can be freely adapted by individual invention.

GENERAL INSTRUCTIONS

1. Pre-wash fabric to prevent further shrinkage and to test for color fastness.
2. Straight grain is the straight line of the thread in the fabric weave.
3. Length grain is along threads parallel to the selvage. Cross grain is along threads which run back

and forth from selvage to selvage. Bias is the diagonal direction between length and cross grain—at 45° to the selvage.

4. Materials in the quilt should all be of a compatible weight and texture.

5. Do not use selvages.

6. Yardages are figured on 45-inch fabric and are approximate only.

7. If the same fabric is to be used in the borders and in piecing the blocks, cut the borders first to be sure of having all the length needed. Use the leftovers for piecing.

8. Use ¼-inch seams for all pieced designs, ¼-inch or ⅛-inch for appliqué. See Notes on Appliqué, p. 88.

9. For any markings that will show on the fabric, use a removable or washable marker. Test first on scraps of the exact fabric being used in the quilt.

10. There are several types and weights of batting. Choose the one most compatible to the fabric and the effect desired. Use only one layer, for a too-thick batting does not permit tiny stitches.

11. Use a small needle for sewing and quilting—7, 8, or 9 "between/quilting" or 9 or 10 "sharp." The "between/quiltings" are all-purpose, the "sharps" are for piecing or appliqué only. Note: the higher the number, the smaller the needle.

12. Cotton thread is preferred by most quilters, especially when working with all-cotton fabric. For piecing, appliquéing, and quilting use a single thread 18 to 20 inches long.

13. Make a sample block to be sure the pattern works well and that your final choice of colors is pleasing.

14. For a choice of nice ways to finish the edges of the quilt, refer to basic quilting manuals.

15. Sign and date the quilt with a permanent marker, *but never a ballpoint or felt-tip pen.* Fine embroidery stitches make the nicest and most lasting signature.

NOTES ON USING PATTERNS

Trace all of the pattern pieces exactly as they are printed, without seam allowance. Transfer them on to a firm art paper—Bristol board for instance—or on to a thin hard plastic. Cut these pieces, called templates, with very sharp scissors or an art knife. Check the final accuracy of the templates by tracing around each one to form an exact replica of the finished block on a piece of paper.

Lay the templates on the wrong side of the fabric, making sure that the grain line marks are straight with the fabric grain. Length grain has slightly less stretch than cross grain, not enough to make a difference in

small pieces. Often the effect of the print—especially a striped print—is the only important factor in deciding between the cross grain and the length grain. Place the pieces far enough apart to allow ¼-inch seams all around each piece. Draw the outline with a sharp pencil—not too dark—staying as close as possible to the template.

Cut ¼ inch away from the outline to allow for seams. If you are timid about cutting an accurate seam allowance, measure and mark at enough points to provide a cutting guide. For total accuracy two sets of templates can be used—one with and one without seam allowances. Trace on the fabric around the larger template first; center the smaller one in the same space and trace around it. Both the seam line and the cutting line will thus be clearly marked on the wrong side of the fabric. If a light pencil has been used, the markings should create no further problem, and will, in fact, be useful when piecing. See Notes on Piecing.

NOTES ON PIECING

If a template without a seam allowance has been used for tracing the shape of each piece on the wrong side of the fabric, as described above, exact seam lines will be clearly marked. Accurate stitching should then be easy. Pin the pieces together, right side to right side, checking to see that the penciled seam lines fall exactly together. If pins are placed across (or perpendicular to) the seam line, they will not be in the way when stitching either by hand or machine.

There is usually an obvious order in which pieces should be joined to form each block. In a four-patch this will mean making four squares, piecing these together to form two strips, and then piecing the strips together to form the whole block. In a nine-patch there will be nine squares formed of smaller pieces, then joined into three strips, and then into a whole block. After each segment is completed, the seams should be pressed to one side. If possible, press toward the darker color so that there will be less chance of a shadow showing through on the right side. With even the best planning it may be necessary to trim edges and corners that may show through.

There are two problem areas in piecing—bias edges and curved edges. Both will cause less trouble if careful attention is paid to the grain line when cutting the fabric. The grain lines on pattern pieces are planned so that long straight edges will fall against long bias ones, thereby preventing distortion of straight lines and making pinning and stitching easier. Keep this same principle in mind when cutting those large triangles for which only dimensions—but no patterns—are given. If curved pieces have been cut with careful attention to grain lines, they will also fit together with a minimum of stretch or pucker. A few more pins are usually required than on straight edges and it is often necessary to clip the concave side at intervals to relieve the strain.

All of the rules for planning, pinning, and pressing also apply when assembling the complete quilt top. Mark seam lines, pay attention to grain, and join units in a convenient order when setting the blocks with sashes, plain blocks, and borders.

NOTES ON APPLIQUÉ

There are several ways to appliqué, and each teacher will stand staunchly by her method. It is often difficult to determine in which way a really fine needle-woman proceeded to appliqué, leading to the conclusion that dedication and practice are more important than method. In either of the two systems most often used the object is the same—to turn under the edge of each piece of appliqué so smoothly that no fold or wrinkle shows along a curve and no loose thread appears at a corner—and to apply the piece to the background fabric with nearly invisible stitches.

One method might be called European and the other Hawaiian. The first method is a little easier to handle and works well with relatively simple shapes such as Hearts, p. 130. The Hawaiian method is almost a must for large intricate designs.

For European appliqué a standard ¼-inch seam allowance can be used. Turn the seam under toward the wrong side of the fabric and finger-crease the edge. It will become obvious that you must make a sharp clip out of the fabric at any deep **V** or concave curve along the edge so that the fabric will lie back smoothly. It may also be necessary to snip away little notches of fabric from corners and convex curves to prevent bulky folds from forming. If finger-creasing is sufficient to hold the edges in place, the piece may then be pinned or basted to the background fabric and finally stitched in place. If the fabric is a little slippery, it may be wise to baste the turned-under edge as you crease it, then pin it to the background fabric.

For the Hawaiian method allow only ⅛-inch seams. Lay the design down smoothly on the background fabric and pin throughout. Then baste, following the outline of the design at a distance of about ⅜ inch in from the raw edge. Turn the edges under with your fingers and the tip of the needle as you sew, clipping where necessary.

A few basic rules apply to either method. Be sure that the design appliqués are not stretched too tightly over the background fabric. A little fullness in the design gives a more three-dimensional effect.

Use a very small blind stitch or slip stitch to hold the edges in place. Never use overcast or whipping stitches except in the deepest **V** where two or three tiny ones may hold stray threads in place. Use matching color thread for each piece. Grandmother often appliquéd with white thread, which may have been all that was available to her. Because of that added problem she was forced to make tiny invisible stitches!

NOTES ON QUILTING

When the quilt top is finished, cut the back and batting larger than the top. Place the backing fabric right-side down on a table; place the batting on top and smooth out any wrinkles. Do not stretch. Then, place the pieced or appliquéd top right-side up on top, thus making a "fabric sandwich." Baste all three layers together, starting from the center and basting out to the edges. Use white or a light-color thread, since black or dark thread may leave traces of dye. Baste from the center up, then from the center down; center to the right edge, then center to the left. Baste the whole quilt in a grid of about six to eight inches, always working from the center to the sides and the center to the top and bottom. Basting on the diagonal may twist or stretch the fabric, so work on the cross grain and lengthwise grain.

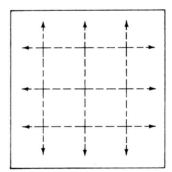

When the basting is completed, the "sandwich" is ready to be quilted. Quilting hoops allow the quilter to be mobile, an important consideration in modern times. Available are several sizes, including 10-, 14-, 18-, and 23-inches in round wood, and small or large in oval wood. The 14-inch and 18-inch round hoops are very easy to manage, but the quilter should choose that size and shape which is most comfortable.

Quilt from the center out. Since the back and batting are larger than the quilt top, any slippage of the top over the edges will be prevented.

Place the inside rim of the hoop on a table. Then, place the center of the basted quilt over the rim. Position the outer rim over the quilt and, while pressing the outer rim down and into place with one hand, keep the other hand inside the rim—palm down—on the quilt, holding the quilt down on the table top. By doing this, some flex will be left in the quilt when the outer rim is tightened in place. Few quilters can quilt with the hoops or floor frames stretched tight; most have difficulty getting the needle in and out in the running stitch of quilting. Some looseness in the fabric is helpful. Be sure the background is smooth. If it is not, remove the hoop and start again.

Concentric Arcs   (Fans)

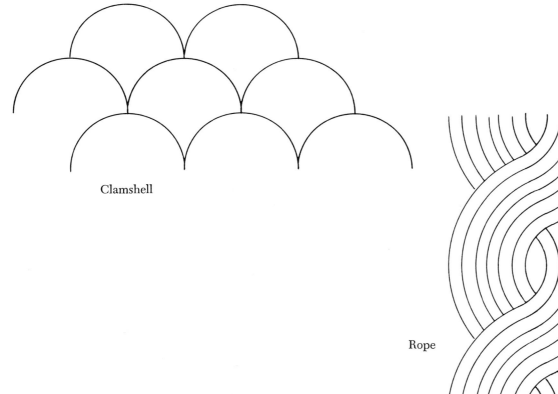

Clamshell

Rope

Princess Feather Wreath

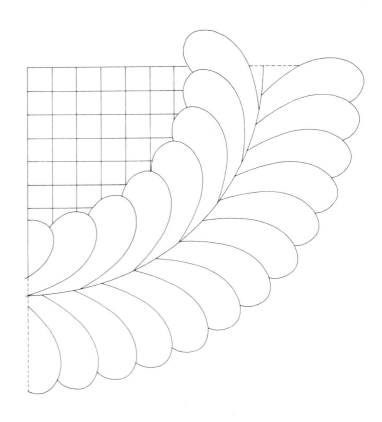

Serpentine   (Princess Feather)

Do not quilt through the basting threads; remove them as you proceed. Work from the center out as for basting—never work the border quilting until all of the central design has been completed out to the border. Before beginning the quilting, bring the edge of the back to the front of the quilt, roll it over the top edges, and baste down. This keeps the edges of the back and the top from raveling, and the batting from fraying.

TRADITIONAL QUILTING DESIGNS

The designs shown here are typical of those seen in quilts of the nineteenth century and are still popular with today's quilters. Full-size templates and instructions for their use are available in shops and by mail order (see p. 91 for mail-order sources). To prepare the quilt for quilting read Notes on Quilting, p. 88, and pay particular attention to point #9 under General Instructions. p. 87.

Suggested mail-order sources for quilting supplies, templates, books, and patterns:

Quilts & Other Comforts
Box 394
Wheatridge, Colorado   80033

Cabin Fever Calicoes
Box 6256
Washington, D.C.   20015

Ginger Snap Station
P.O. Box 81086
Atlanta, Georgia   30341

Mrs. Wigg's Cabbage Patch, Inc.
2600 Beaver Avenue
Des Moines, Iowa   50310

The Silver Thimble
249 High Street
Ipswich, Massachusetts   01938

The Quiltworks
218 3rd Avenue
Minneapolis, Minnesota   55401

Quilt Country
500 Nichols Road
Kansas City, Missouri   64112

Mail-in
P.O. Box 603
Woodcliff Lake, New Jersey   07675

Gutcheon Patchworks
611 Broadway
New York, N.Y.   10012

Cross Patch
Rt. #9
Garrison, New York   10524

Creative Quilt Center
Stearns & Foster
Box 15380
Cincinnati, Ohio 45215

Contemporary Quilts
3466 Summer Avenue
Memphis, Tennessee   38122

Great Expectations
155 Town and County Village
Houston, Texas 77024

Let's Quilt and Sew-on
P.O. Box 29526
San Antonio, Texas   78229

Calico Country Store
10822 124th Street
Edmonton, Alberta
Canada   T5M 0H3

Suggested books for beginners:

The Perfect Patchwork Primer
by Beth Gutcheon
David McKay Company, Inc.
750 3rd Avenue
New York, N.Y. 10017

Quick and Easy Quilting
by Bonnie Leman
Moon Over the Mountain Publishing
   Company
6700 West 44th Avenue
Wheatridge, Colorado 80033

You Can Be a Super Quilter
by Carla Hassel
Wallace-Homestead Book Company
1912 Grand Avenue
Des Moines, Iowa 50305

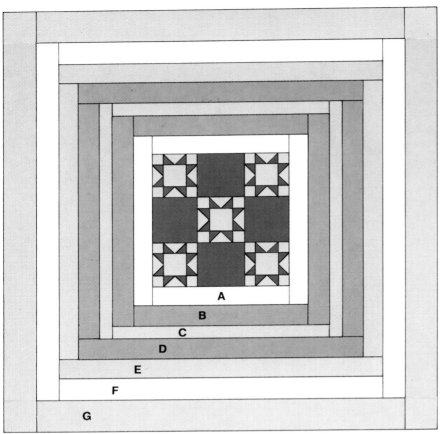

Diagram of quilt illustrated in figure 49

STAR MEDALLION

Dimensions: 33 x 33 inches.

Materials: all 45-inch fabrics.

¼ yard dark red
1 yard yellow—includes borders #C and #G
⅞ yard blue print
⅝ yard medium red print
¾ yard light red
⅞ yard red check

Cut: Add ¼-inch seam allowance all around each piece and to each measurement given.

5 yellow #1
20 yellow #2
20 yellow #3
40 dark red #4
4 dark red 4-inch squares
2 blue print A-border strips, top and bottom, 1½ x 12 inches.
2 blue print A-border strips, sides, 1½ x 15 inches.
2 medium red print B-border strips, top and bottom, 1½ x 15 inches.

2 medium red print B-border strips, sides, 1½ x 18 inches.
2 yellow C-border strips, top and bottom, 1 x 18 inches.
2 yellow C-border strips, sides, 1 x 20 inches.
2 light red D-border strips, top and bottom, 1½ x 23 inches.
2 light red D-border strips, sides, 1½ x 20 inches.
2 red check E-border strips, top and bottom. 1½ x 26 inches.
2 red check E-border strips, sides, 1½ x 23 inches.
2 blue print F-border strips, top and bottom, 1½ x 26 inches.
2 blue print F-border strips, sides, 1½ x 29 inches.
2 yellow G-border strips, top and bottom, 2 x 29 inches.
2 yellow G-border strips, sides, 2 x 33 inches.

Directions: Cut out and piece the five Star blocks, as shown. Set them together with the four plain squares and add the seven sets of borders.

Full-size pattern pieces
Add seam allowances

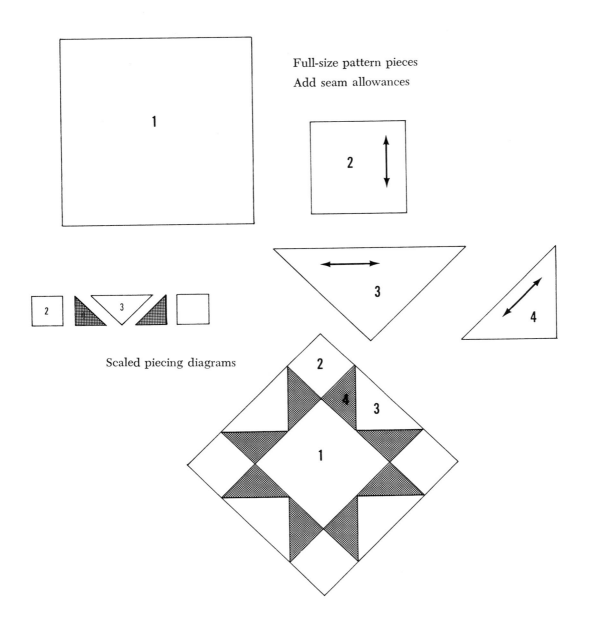

1

2

3

4

2   3

Scaled piecing diagrams

2

4   3

1

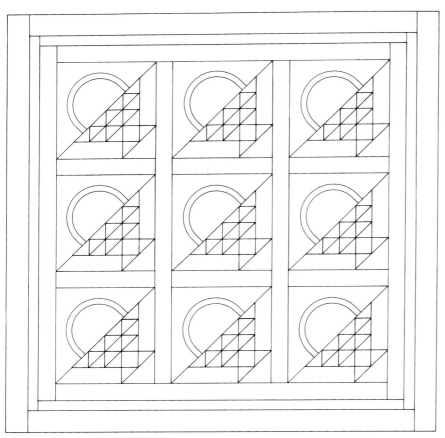

Diagram of quilt illustrated in figure 52

BASKETS

Dimensions: 44 x 44 inches.

Materials: All 45-inch fabrics.

   2 yards light
   ½ yard medium
   1¼ yards dark
   1½ yards backing
   ½ yard for binding, or use scraps of light

Cut: Add ¼-inch seam allowance all around each piece and to each measurement given.

For each block: Total:
   1 light #1   9 pieces
  11 dark #2   99 pieces
   5 medium #2   45 pieces
   1 light #3   9 pieces
   1 light #4   9 pieces
   1 light #4 reversed   9 pieces
 14 inches medium bias,
    width of #5, for each handle   126 inches
   1 large light triangle—

10 inches on right-angle sides, and straight grain on short sides.   9 pieces

For settings and borders:
   6 light sash strips, 2 x 10 inches.
   2 light sash strips, 2 x 34 inches.
   2 light inner-border strips, top and bottom,
     2 x 34 inches.
   2 light inner-border strips, sides, 2 x 38 inches.
   2 dark second-border strips, top and bottom,
     1 x 38 inches.
   2 dark second-border strips, sides, 1 x 40 inches.
   2 light outer-border strips, top and bottom,
     2 x 40 inches.
   2 light outer-border strips, sides, 2 x 44 inches.

Directions: Piece the Basket blocks as shown in the diagram. Set them together in three vertical rows with the short sash strips between. Set the rows together with the long sash strips between. Add the three sets of borders.

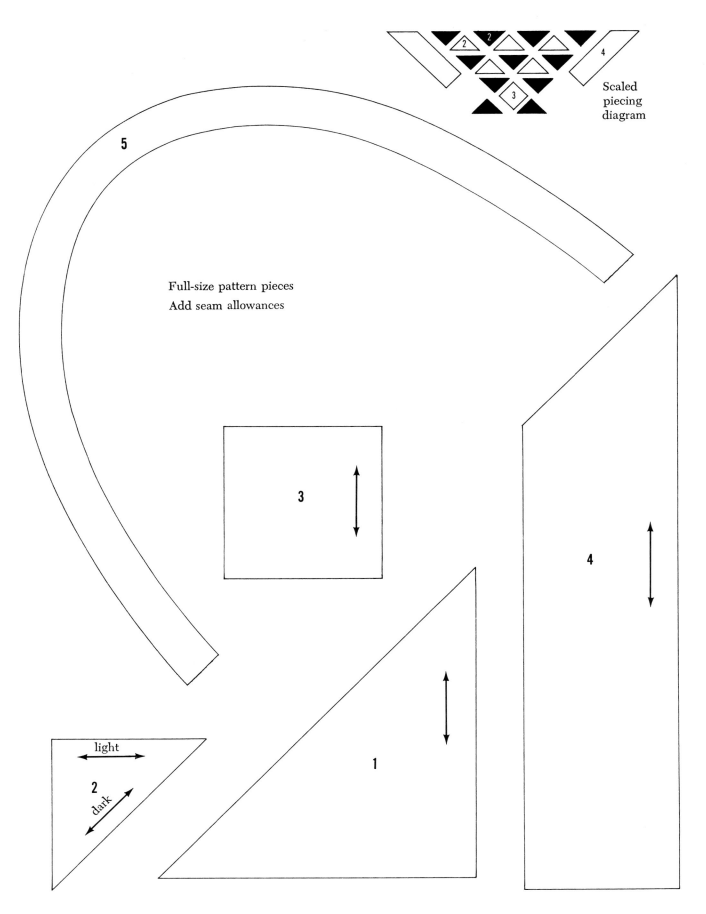

Scaled piecing diagram

Full-size pattern pieces
Add seam allowances

5

3

4

light

2
dark

1

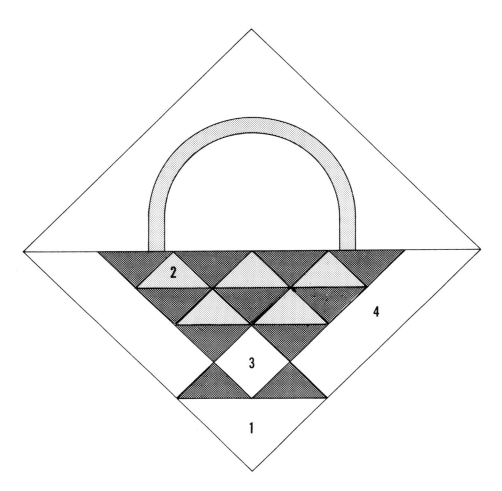

Scaled piecing diagram

SCHOOLHOUSE

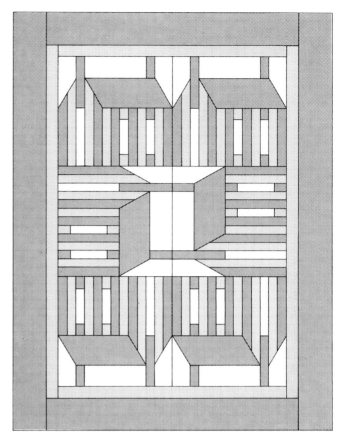

Diagram of quilt illustrated in figure 58

Dimensions: 27½ x 37¼ inches.

Materials: all 45-inch fabrics.
   1¼ yards red—includes binding
   1 yard blue
   ¾ yard white
   1 yard backing

Cut: Add ¼-inch seam allowance all around each piece and to each measurement given.

   6 each white #3, #4, #9, #14, #21, #23
   6 each blue #2, #7, #10, #11, #13, #17, #20
   6 each red #1, #5, #6, #8, #12, #15, #16, #18, #19, #22

2 blue inner-border strips, top and bottom,
   1 x 19½ inches.
2 blue inner-border strips, sides, 1 x 31¼ inches.
2 red outer-border strips, top and bottom,
   3 x 21½ inches.
2 red outer-border strips, sides, 3 x 37¼ inches.

Directions: When piecing the house block, break it down into workable sections, then join the sections. Piece according to the diagrams, being very careful of exact seam allowances, so that all segments will fit to form a smooth block 9¾ inches square. Set the six blocks together as shown and add the two sets of borders. You may wish to round the corners, as in the original quilt, before binding.

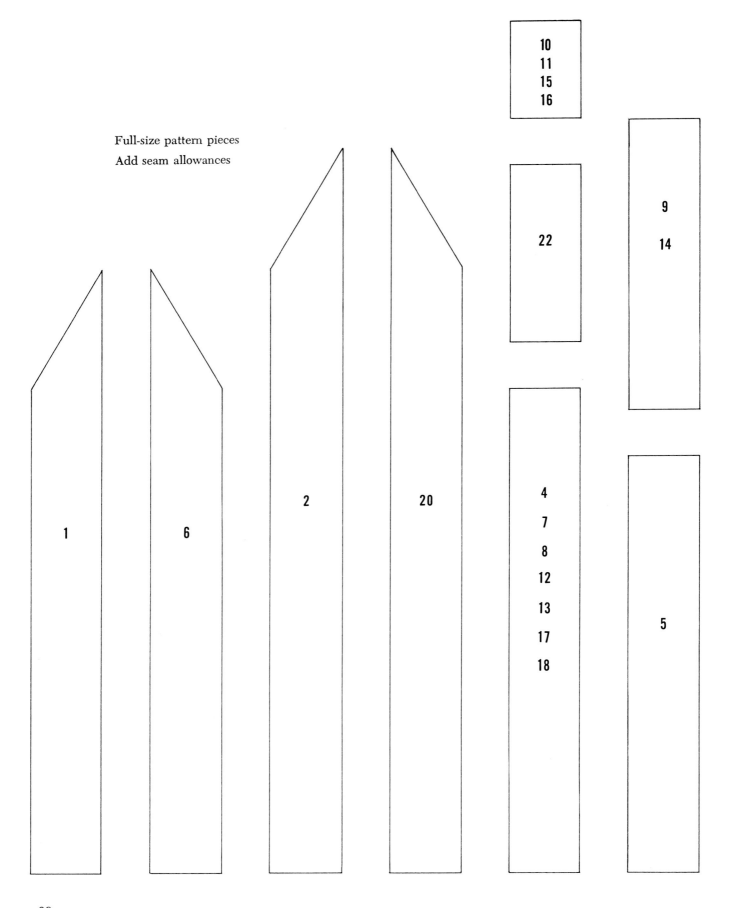

Full-size pattern pieces
Add seam allowances

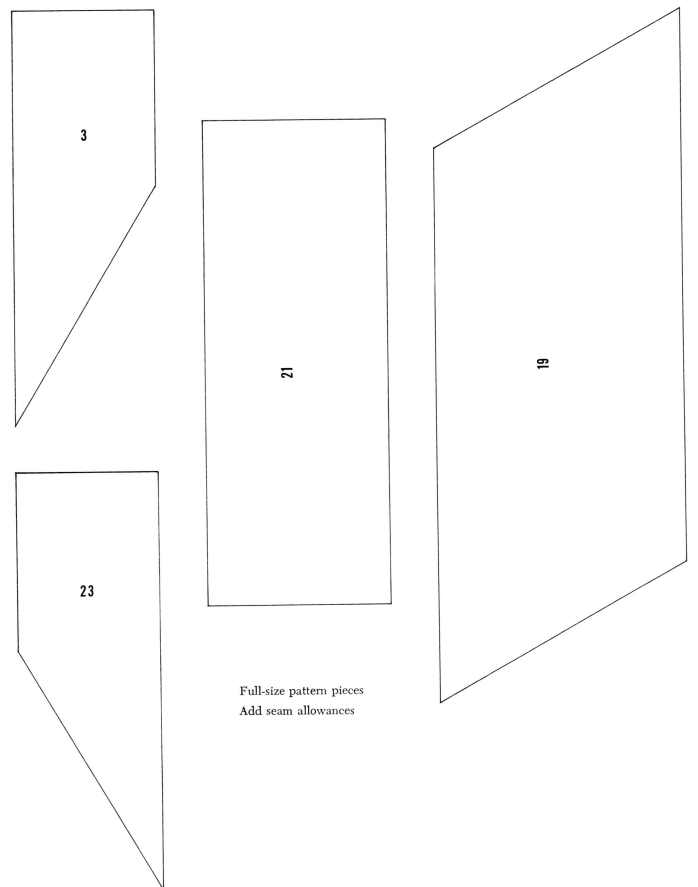

3

21

19

23

Full-size pattern pieces
Add seam allowances

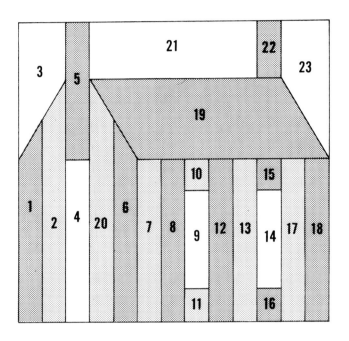

Scaled piecing diagram

CIRCUS

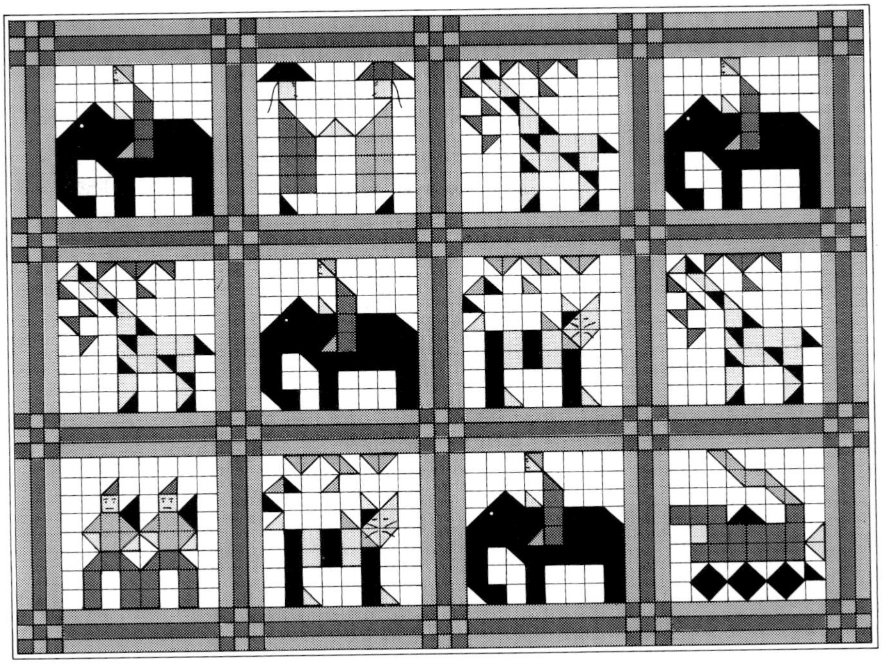

Diagram of quilt illustrated in figure 60

Dimensions: 33 x 43¼ inches.

Materials: all 45-inch fabrics.

For piecing figures:
  1¼ yards white—includes binding
  ⅜ yard black
  ⅜ yard dark red
  ¼ yard bright blue
  ¼ yard tan
  ⅛ yard gold

For other areas:
  1 yard red
  ¾ yard green
  1½ yards backing

Cut: Add ¼-inch seam allowance all around each piece and to each measurement given.

The number of #1 and #2 pieces in the colors shown for each block. See diagram that also provides the total number of pieces in each color. Note that each picture block contains a total of 64 squares.

  100 green #3 corner blocks
   80 red #3 corner blocks
   31 green #4 sashes
   62 red #4 sashes

Directions: Piece each block together, following carefully the arrangements in the diagrams. Piece twenty checkerboard corner blocks. Piece thirty-one sashes of two red strips and one green strip each. Assemble the quilt by alternating the picture blocks and sashes, and finish it with borders of sashes and corner blocks.

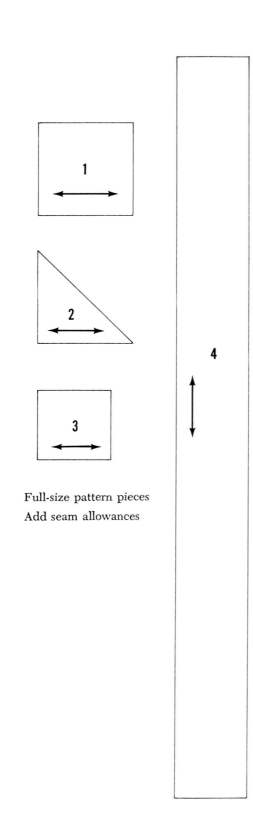

Full-size pattern pieces

Add seam allowances

Giraffe
    34 pieces white #1
    7 pieces tan #1
    17 pieces white #2
    10 pieces black #2
    10 pieces tan #2
    9 pieces red #2

Chinamen
    34 pieces white #1
    8 pieces red #1
    7 pieces blue #1
    2 pieces gold #1
    1 piece black #1
    12 pieces white #2
    4 pieces red #2
    4 pieces black #2
    2 pieces gold #2
    2 pieces blue #2

Elephant
    28 pieces white #1
    23 pieces black #1
    3 pieces red #1
    8 pieces white #2
    7 pieces black #2
    2 pieces gold #2
    2 pieces blue #2
    1 piece red #2

Twins
    32 pieces white #1
    10 pieces red #1
    4 pieces blue #1
    2 pieces gold #1
    12 pieces white #2
    6 pieces blue #2
    6 pieces red #2
    4 pieces gold #2
    4 pieces black #2

Steam Locomotive
    24 pieces white #1
    15 pieces red #1
    1 piece blue #1
    1 piece gold #1
    23 pieces white #2
    15 pieces black #2
    6 pieces blue #2
    2 pieces gold #2

Cat
    31 pieces white #1
    9 pieces black #1
    5 pieces gold (or tan) #1
    17 pieces white #2
    10 pieces blue #2
    8 pieces gold (or tan) #2
    3 pieces black #2

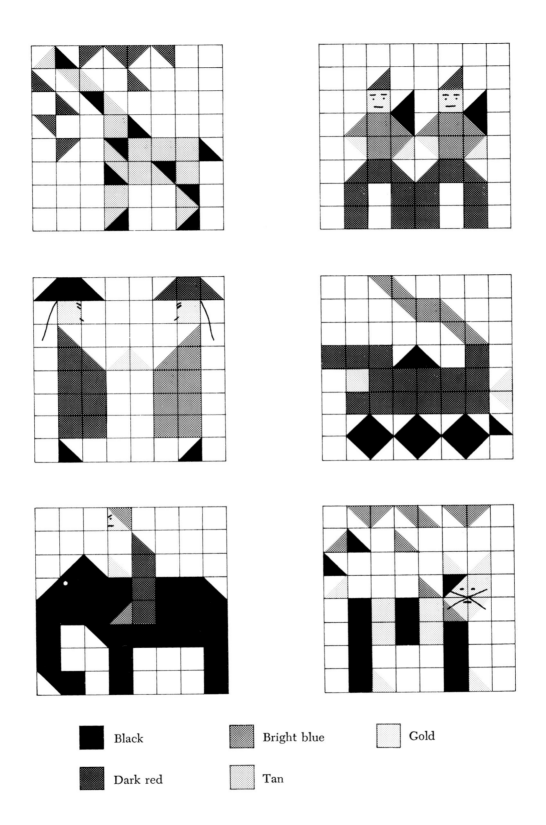

Black

Bright blue

Gold

Dark red

Tan

LONE STAR

Diagram of quilt
illustrated in figure 63

Dimensions: 40¾ x 44¾ inches.

Materials: all 45-inch fabrics.

  1⅜ yards white
  1¼ yards medium blue—includes inner border and
    binding
  ⅛ yard rose
  ⅛ yard gold
  ⅛ yard palest pink
  ⅛ yard yellow
  ¼ yard navy
  ⅛ yard purple
  ⅛ yard lavender
  ⅛ yard pale pink
  ⅛ yard medium pink
  1½ yards backing

*Cut: Add ¼-inch seam allowance all around each piece
and to each measurement given.*

For each large diamond (using small diamond pattern):

		Total
2	rose	16
2	gold	16
3	palest pink	24
4	yellow	32
5	medium blue	40
6	navy	48
5	purple	40
4	lavender	32
3	pale pink	24
2	medium pink	16

For settings and borders:
  4 white 9-inch squares
  4 white triangles—9 inches on each right-angle side,
    and the straight grain on long side.
  2 medium blue inner-border strips, top and bottom,
    2 x 30¾ inches.
  2 medium blue inner-border strips, sides,
    2 x 34¾ inches.
  2 white outer-border strips, top and bottom,
    5 x 34¾ inches.
  2 white outer-border strips, sides, 3 x 44¾ inches.

Directions: Working in diagonal rows, and following
the color diagram and the picture of the original quilt
in figure 63 (beginning and ending with a rose piece
at each point), join the thirty-six pieces made of ten
colors to form one large diamond. Make eight diamonds and join them together to form a Star. Set the
four large triangles and four large squares between
the points of the Star so as to frame the Star. Add the
two sets of borders.

Full-size pattern piece
Add seam allowances

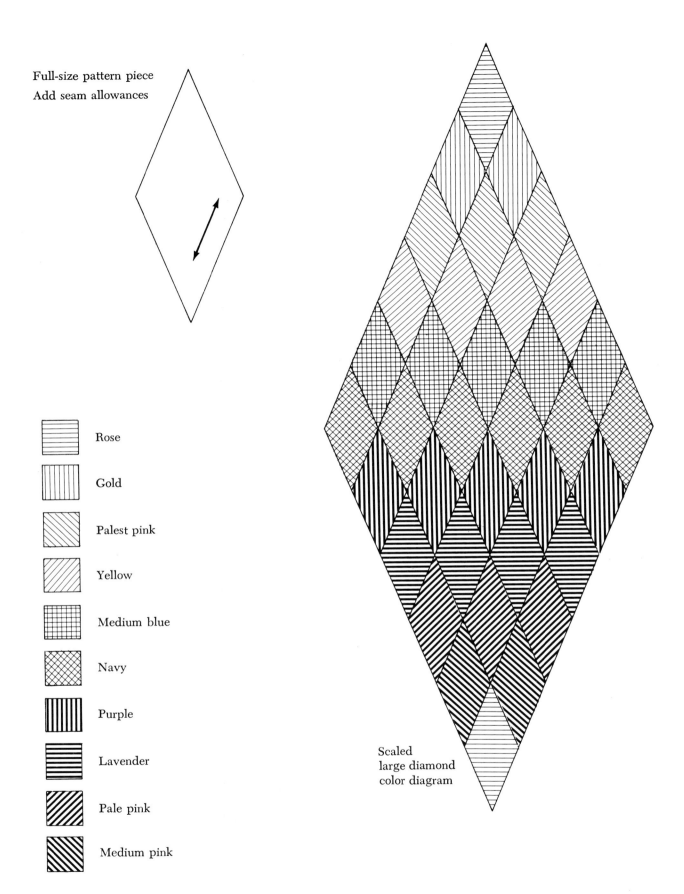

Rose

Gold

Palest pink

Yellow

Medium blue

Navy

Purple

Lavender

Pale pink

Medium pink

Scaled
large diamond
color diagram

Diagram of quilt illustrated in figure 81

TULIP CROSS APPLIQUÉ

Dimensions: 42 x 42 inches.

Materials: all 45-inch fabrics.

   1¾ yards white—includes binding
   1 yard dark green
   ¾ yard red
   ½ yard gold
   1¼ yards backing

Cut: Add ¼- or ⅛-inch (see Notes on Appliqué) all around each piece and to each measurement given.

   1 dark green #1
   4 dark green #4
   8 dark green #5
   4 dark green #7 and 4 reversed
   4 dark green #8 and 4 reversed
   4 dark green #9 and 4 reversed
  12 dark green #14

   1 red #3
   8 red #6
   4 red #10 and 4 reversed
   4 red #12
  16 red #15
   1 gold #2
   4 gold #11 and 4 reversed
   4 gold #13
   3 yards dark green bias, ⅜ inch wide, for stems.

Directions: Prepare the background fabric by cutting a 42-inch square on the grain. Fold and crease it from side to side, top to bottom, and corner to corner, as shown in the small diagram. Use the creases as guide lines for placing each piece. Appliqué the pieces to the background, overlapping the flowers over the raw ends of the stems, and so forth.

Scaled piecing diagram (one-fourth of quilt)

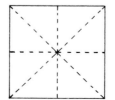

Folding diagram

15

5

6

13

14

8

7

Full-size pattern pieces   Add seam allowances

108

4

Full-size pattern piece
Add seam allowances

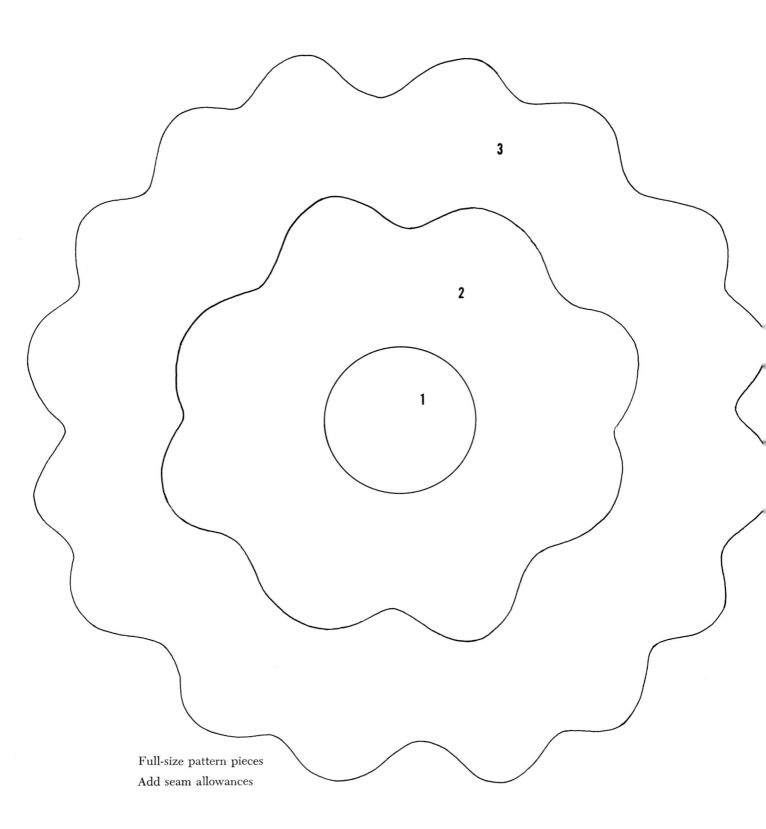

3

2

1

Full-size pattern pieces
Add seam allowances

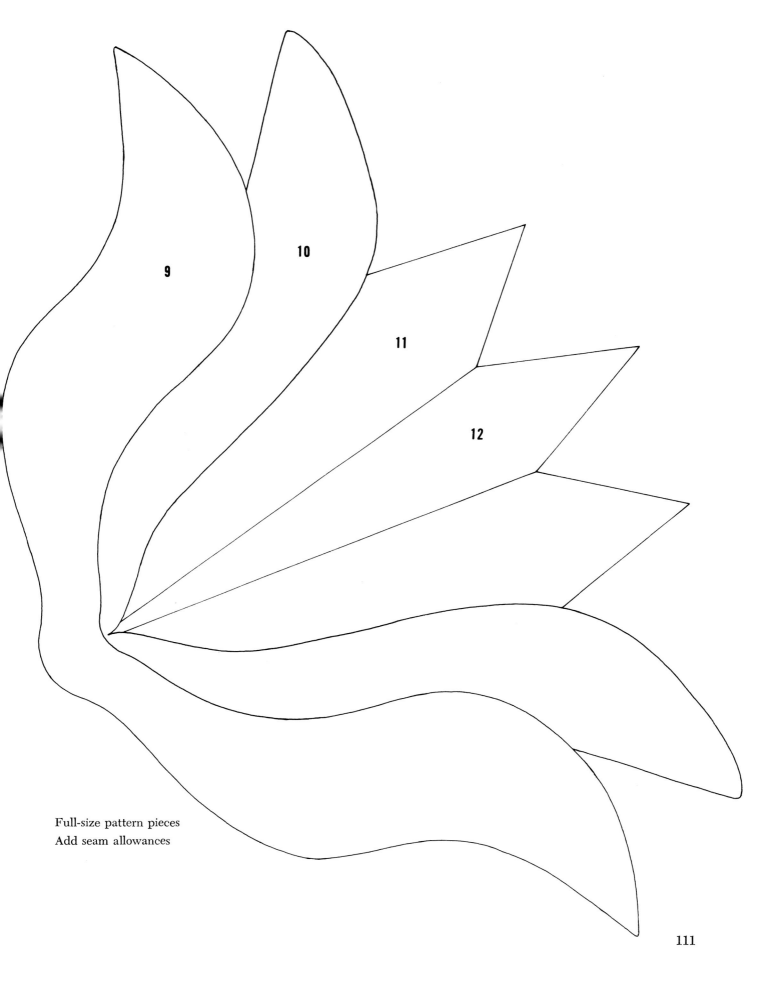

9

10

11

12

Full-size pattern pieces
Add seam allowances

Diagram of quilt illustrated in figure 91

FLORAL APPLIQUÉ

Dimensions: 44 x 44 inches.

Materials: all 45-inch fabrics

    1¾ yards light
    ¾ yard dark—includes binding
    1½ yards backing

Cut: Add ¼-inch seam allowance all around each piece and to each measurement given.

    1 light square, 24 x 24 inches.
    4 large dark flowers
    5 small dark flowers
    4 light centers for large flowers (optional)
    5 light centers for small flowers (optional)
  52 dark triangles
  52 light triangles

2 light border strips, tops and bottoms, 8 x 28 inches.
2 light border strips, sides, 8 x 44 inches.

Directions: Fold the large square twice diagonally from corner to corner. Place the small flower at the center point. Place each of the large flowers on one of the diagonal lines at the same distance from the center flower as shown. Note: the flower centers may be made by cutting a circle from the center of each flower and appliquéing around it so that the background fabric shows through the center hole, or by placing a small circular piece of fabric on top of the center of each flower and appliquéing it in place.

Piece the Sawtooth border, using any one of the three arrangements shown in the diagrams, and attach it to the finished center block. Attach the plain border strips and place the four small flowers evenly in each of the four corners as shown.

Full-size pattern pieces
Add seam allowances

Border diagram A

Full-size pattern pieces
Add seam allowances

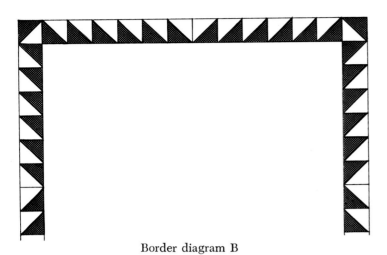

Border diagram B

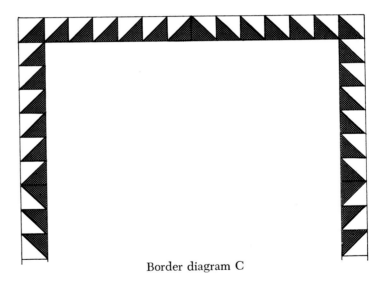

Border diagram C

▨	Purple	▥	Wine red
▦	Magenta	▧	Raspberry
☐	Cream	▥	Light purple

Diagram of quilt illustrated in figure 100

GRANDMOTHER'S DREAM

Dimensions: 43 x 43 inches.

Materials: all 45-inch fabrics.

⅞ yard wine red—includes inner border
¼ yard cream
⅜ yard raspberry red—includes outer corner squares
1 yard magenta—includes outer border
¼ yard purple
½ yard light purple
1½ yards backing
½ yard fabric for binding—can be chosen from any of the above colors

Cut: Add ¼-inch seam allowance all around each piece and to each measurement given.

17 purple #1
24 magenta #1
36 cream #1
12 wine red #1
24 raspberry #1
28 wine red #2
4 wine red #3
4 large light-purple triangles—12 inches on right-angle sides, and straight grain on the long side.
2 wine red inner-border strips, top and bottom, 4 x 32 inches.
2 wine red inner-border strips, sides, 4 x 24 inches.
4 magenta outer-border strips, 7 x 32 inches.
4 raspberry outer-corner squares, 7 x 7 inches.

Directions: Piece the center diamond, following the color key. Add the four large triangles to form a square. Add the inner-border strips. Join the outer-corner squares to the outer-border strips and add that border to the quilt.

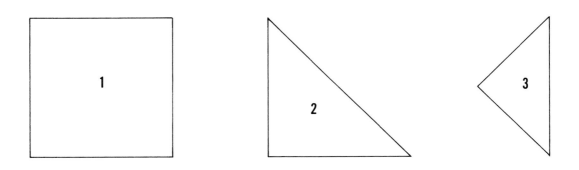

Full-size pattern pieces   Add seam allowances

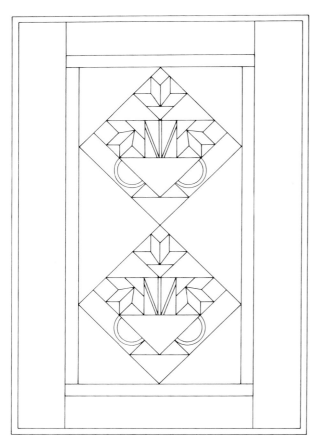

Diagram of quilt illustrated in figure 108

CAROLINA LILY

Dimensions: 34 x 50 inches.

Materials: all 45-inch fabrics.

    1¾ yards medium brown
    ½ yard gold
    ¼ yard dark green
    1¼ yards purple
    1½ yards backing

Cut: Add ¼-inch seam allowance all around each piece and to each measurement given.

  24 gold #1
  12 medium brown #2
   6 medium brown #3
   6 dark green #4
   4 medium brown #5
   2 medium brown #6
   2 gold #7
   4 gold #8
   2 medium brown #9
   4 medium brown #10

   4 gold 7½-inch bias strips for #11
   6 dark green 5½-inch bias strips for #12
   4 medium brown corner triangles—10 inches on the right angle sides, and straight grain on the long side.
   2 medium brown side triangles—14 inches on the right angle sides, and straight grain on the long side.
   2 purple inner-border strips, top and bottom, 2 x 24 inches.
   2 purple inner-border strips, sides, 2 x 40 inches.
   2 medium brown outer-border strips, top and bottom, 3 x 24 inches.
   2 medium brown outer-border strips, sides, 5 x 50 inches.

Directions: Piece the Lily blocks as shown in the diagram. Position them point-to-point as shown and frame them with the two side triangles and the four corner triangles. Add the two sets of borders.

118

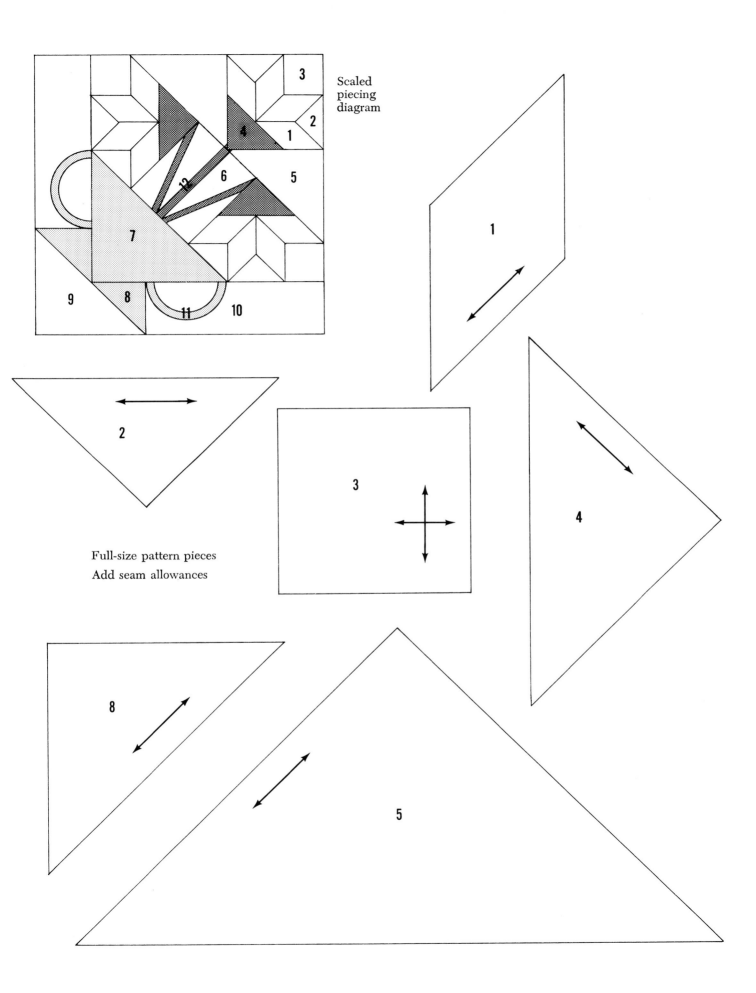

Scaled piecing diagram

Full-size pattern pieces
Add seam allowances

Full-size pattern pieces
Add seam allowances

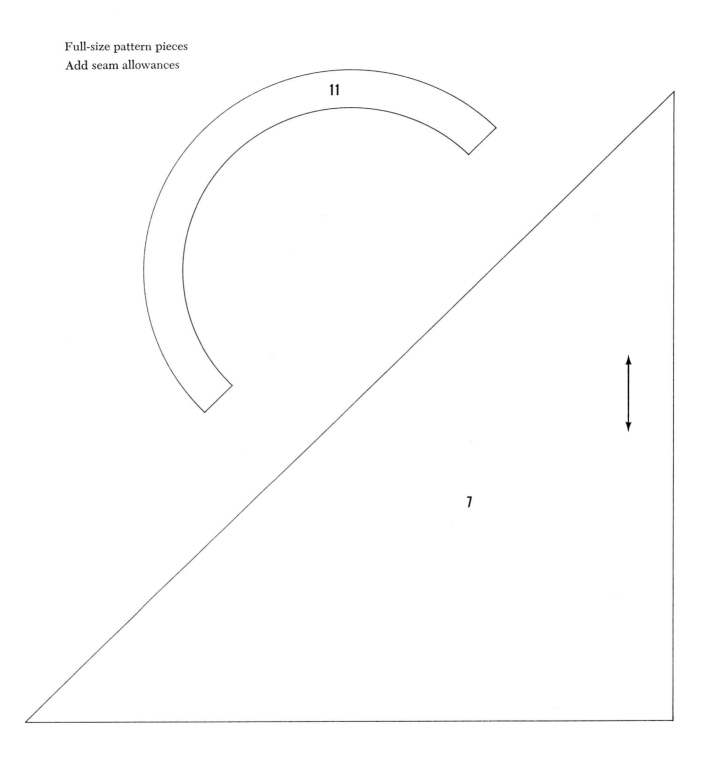

11

7

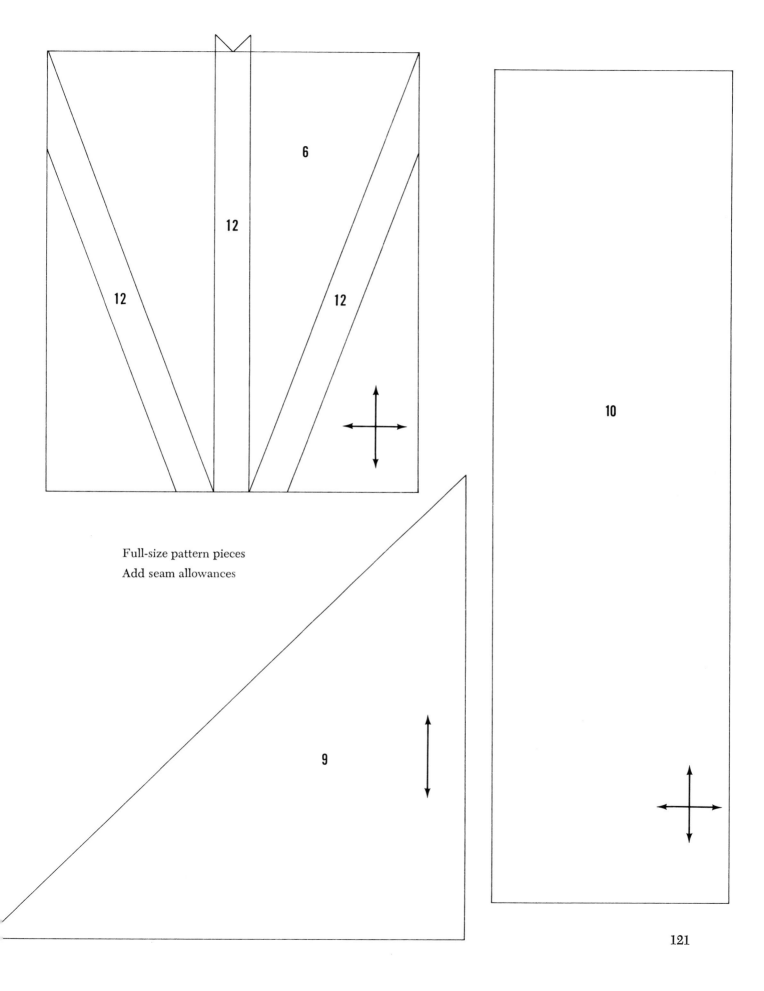

Full-size pattern pieces
Add seam allowances

6

12

12

12

10

9

Diagram of quilt illustrated in figure 109

BEAR'S PAW

Dimensions: 33 x 35 inches.

Materials: all 45-inch fabrics.

- 1⅛ yards dark
- ¾ yard light
- ⅛ to ¼ yard several colors (or scraps) for piecing blocks
- 1⅛ yards backing
- ½ yard for binding or use scraps of light

Cut: Add ¼-inch seam allowance all around each piece and to each measurement given.

For each block:	Total:
4 one color #1	36 pieces
16 same color #2	144 pieces
1 same color #3	9 pieces
4 contrast color #3	36 pieces
4 same contrast #4	36 pieces

For setting:
- 4 dark #5
- 8 dark #6
- 4 dark #7
- 2 light inner-border strips, top and bottom, 2 x 21 inches.
- 2 light inner-border strips, sides, 2 x 25 inches.
- 2 dark outer-border strips, top and bottom, 5 x 25 inches.
- 2 dark outer-border strips, sides, 4 x 35 inches.

Directions: Piece the Bear's Paw blocks as shown in diagram A. Set the pieced blocks diagonally with the plain blocks and triangles as shown in diagram B. Add the two sets of borders.

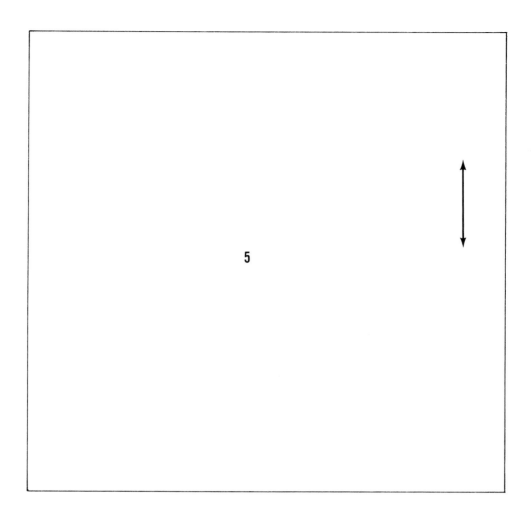

Full-size pattern piece   Add seam allowances

Scaled piecing diagram A

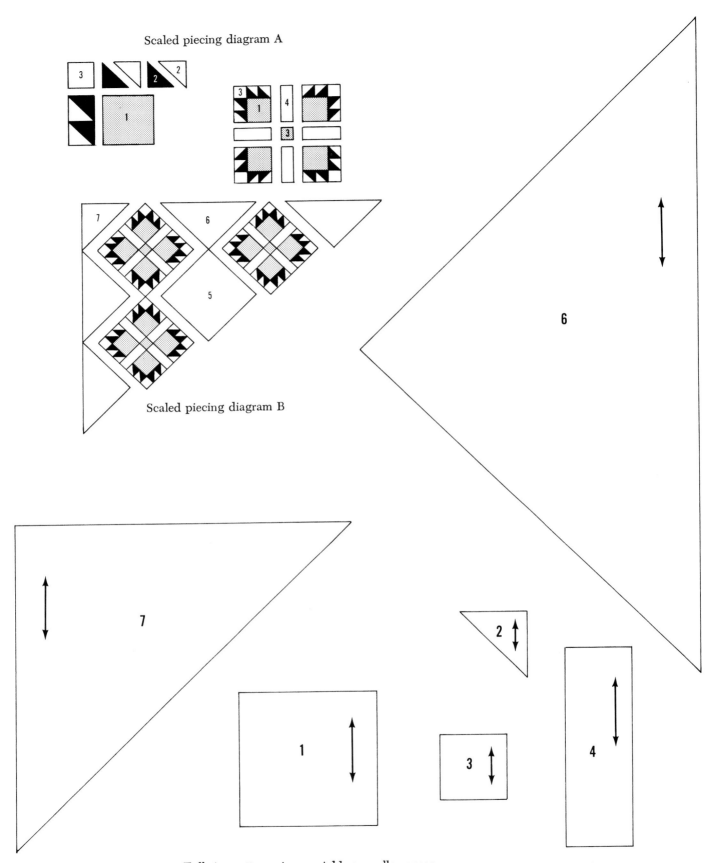

Scaled piecing diagram B

Full-size pattern pieces   Add seam allowances

TUMBLING BLOCKS

Diagram of quilt illustrated in figure 112

Dimensions: 40¼ x 50½ inches.

Materials: all 45-inch fabrics.

   1½ yards dark
   1¼ yards medium
   ¾ yard light—includes binding
   1½ yards backing

Cut: Add ¼-inch seam allowance all around each piece and to each measurement given.

   60 dark #1
   60 medium #1
   50 light #1
   10 light #2
    8 light #3
    2 light #4 and 2 reversed
    2 medium border strips, top and bottom,
       2 x 26¼ inches.
    2 medium border strips, sides, 2 x 41½ inches.
    2 dark border strips, top and bottom, 5 x 30¼ inches.
    2 dark border strips, sides, 5 x 51½ inches.

Directions: Join medium and dark #1 pieces together, leaving the seam open at the V. Seam the light piece into the V, turning the corner sharply where the seam was left open. Set all the blocks together and add the #2, #3, and #4 pieces to form the complete center rectangle. Add the two sets of borders.

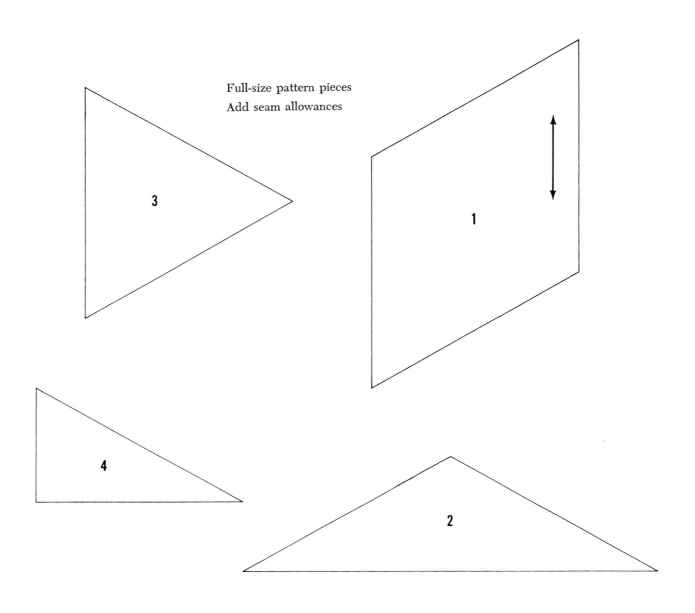

Full-size pattern pieces
Add seam allowances

3

1

4

2

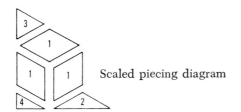

Scaled piecing diagram

DOUBLE WEDDING RING

(For advanced quilters)

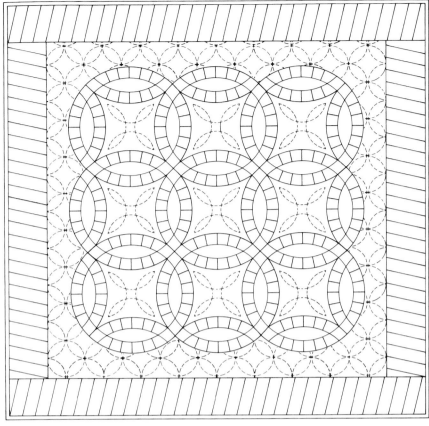

Diagram of quilt illustrated in figure 123

Dimensions: 56 x 56 inches.

Materials: all 45-inch fabrics.

    1⅜ yards red
    1 yard black
    ⅛ yard each or scraps of 13 colors (see color key)
    1¾ yards backing

Cut: Add ¼-inch seam allowance all around each piece and to each measurement given.

    24 black #4
    9 black #5
    24 peach #3
    24 pink #3
    48 royal blue #2
    24 lavender #2
    24 green #2
    24 #1 in each of the other eight colors
    48-inch red background square

Pieced borders are made up of 1¾-inch strips. Total top and bottom size: 4 x 56 inches; total side size: 4 x 48 inches.

The borders may be pieced more efficiently in one strip, 56 x 20 inches, then cut apart into the sizes given.

Directions: Following the color key, join four #1 pieces in a curved row. Add a #2 piece to each end. Make up twenty-four of these and another twenty-four to which #3 pieces are joined at the ends. To each of these constructions next join a #4 piece to form a complete melon shape, as shown in the diagram. Join the completed melon shapes to the four sides of five #5 pieces, which form the center and the four corners of the completed Wedding Ring motif. Add the last four #5 pieces and melon shapes to the top and bottom and both sides and appliqué the entire construction on to the red background square. Cut away the background fabric from behind the Wedding Rings to reduce bulk. Add the completed borders to the red center block.

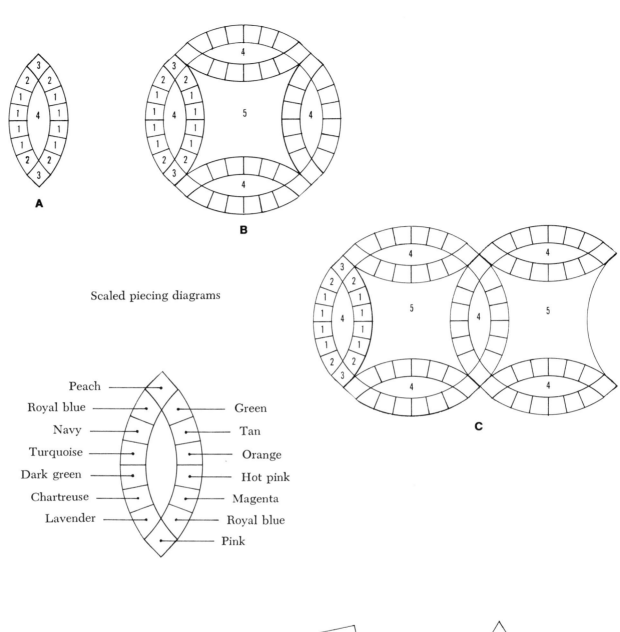

Scaled piecing diagrams

Peach —
Royal blue —
Navy —
Turquoise —
Dark green —
Chartreuse —
Lavender —

— Green
— Tan
— Orange
— Hot pink
— Magenta
— Royal blue
— Pink

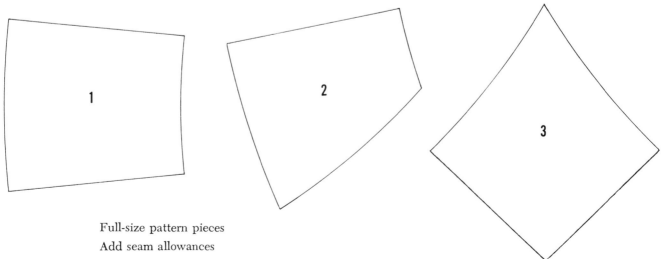

Full-size pattern pieces
Add seam allowances

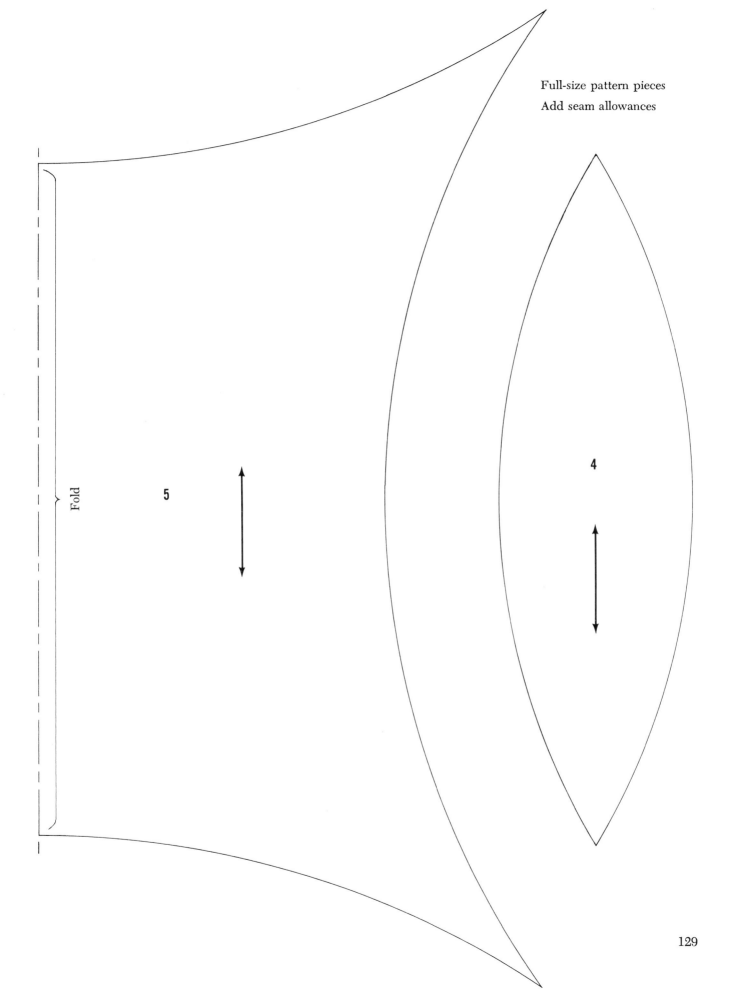

Full-size pattern pieces
Add seam allowances

Fold

5

4

129

Diagram of quilt illustrated in figure 152

HEARTS DOLL QUILT

Dimensions: 19 x 20½ inches.

Materials: all 45-inch fabrics.

⅓ yard white
⅝ yard checked gingham
⅛ yard several colors or scraps for hearts

Cut: Add ¼-inch seam allowance all around each piece and to each measurement given.

36 white #1
36 assorted #2
 2 gingham border strips, top and bottom, 2 x 19 inches.
 2 gingham border strips, sides, 2 x 16½ inches.

Directions: Appliqué one #2 piece in the center of each #1 piece. Sew the blocks together in rows, then join the rows to form the whole center section. Add the border pieces.

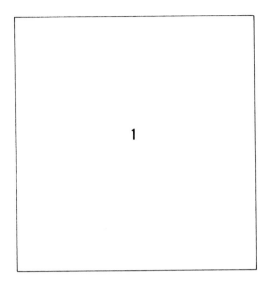

Full-size pattern pieces
Add seam allowances

NOTES

1. Phyllis Cunnington and Catherine Lucas, *Costume for Births, Marriages and Deaths* (New York: Barnes & Noble Books, 1972), p. 19, citing J. C. Cox, *Parish Register of England,* 1910.

2. George Frederic Still, *The History of Paediatrics: The Progress of the Study of Diseases of Children up to the End of the XVIIIth Century* (London: Oxford University Press, 1931; reprint ed., London: Dawsons of Pall Mall, 1965), pp. 31–32.

3. *Ibid.,* p. 64.

4. *Ibid.,* p. 264.

5. *Ibid.,* pp. 379–380.

6. Patsy and Myron Orlofsky, *Quilts in America* (New York: McGraw-Hill Book Company, 1974), p. 35. The Orlofskys are quoting from Alice Morse Earle, *Customs and Fashions in Old New England.*

7. Marie D. Webster, *Quilts: Their Story and How to Make Them* (New York: Doubleday, Page, 1915), p. 53.

8. Still, *History of Paediatrics,* p. 451.

9. *Ibid.,* p. 422.

10. Dick, "The Clothing of Children," *The Family Magazine 4* (1837), pp. 461–462, quoted in Bernard Wishy, *The Child and the Republic* (Philadelphia: University of Pennsylvania Press, 1968), p. 38.

11. Anita Schorsch, *Images of Childhood* (New York: Mayflower Books, 1979), pp. 11, 169.

12. *Ibid.,* pp. 14–15.

13. Still, *History of Paediatrics,* p. 64.

14. Schorsch, *Images of Childhood,* p. 17.

15. Still, *History of Paediatrics,* p. 169.

16. Schorsch, *Images of Childhood,* pp. 12–14, 17, 29.

17. *Ibid.,* pp. 130–149, 164.

18. Described by Julia de Wolf Addison in Webster, *Quilts: Their Story,* p. 39.

19. Elizabeth Glaister, *Needlework* (London: Macmillan & Co., 1880), p. 96.

20. Averil Colby, *Quilting* (New York: Charles Scribner's Sons, 1971), p. 87.

21. Mavis Fitzrandolph, *Traditional Quilting: Its Story and Its Practice* (London: B.T. Batsford, 1954), p. 19.

22. Victoria and Albert Museum, Department of Textiles, *Notes on Quilting* (London: Board of Education, Kynoch Press, 1932), plates 4, 6, 13.

23. Fitzrandolph, *Traditional Quilting,* p. 74.

24. R. B. Bailey, "Pilgrim Possessions," manuscript copy, Henry N. Flynt Library of Historic Deerfield, Inc., Deerfield, Massachusetts, 1951.

25. Abbott Lowell Cummings, *Rural Household Inventories, 1675–1775* (Boston: The Society of the Preservation of New England Antiquities, 1964), pp. xiii–xl.

26. Bailey, "Pilgrim Possessions," p. 45.

27. Cummings, *Rural Household Inventories, 1675–1775,* pp. 54–57.

28. *Ibid.,* p. 8.

29. *Ibid.,* p. 117.

30. *Ibid.,* p. 78.

31. *Ibid.,* p. 163.

32. Alice Morse Earle, *Customs and Fashions in Old New England* (New York: Charles Scribner's Sons, 1893), pp. 1–4.

33. Katharine Morrison McClinton, *Antiques of American Childhood* (New York: Clarkson N. Potter, 1970), p. 38.

34. "Diary of Eliza Babcock Leonard," Greenfield, Massachusetts, August 19, 1841–June 13, 1850, manuscript copy in the collection of the Pocumtuck Valley Memorial Association, Deerfield, Massachusetts.

35. Catharine Esther Beecher and Harriet Beecher Stowe, *The American Woman's Home: or, Principles of Domestic Science* (New York: J.B. Ford, 1869), p. 269.

36. Cummings, *Rural Household Inventories, 1675–1775,* p. 3.

37. *Ibid.,* p. 5.

38. Marion L. Channing, ed., *Laura Russell Remembers* (New Bedford, Mass.: Reynolds-DeWalt Printing, 1970), p. 13.

39. Inventory listing for William Ascough of Westchester City, 1785, at The New-York Historical Society, New York.

40. Lilian Baker Carlisle, *18th & 19th Century American Art at Shelburne Museum,* Museum Pamphlet Series, no. 5 (Shelburne, Vt.: Shelburne Museum, 1960).

41. Margaret E. White, *Quilts and Counterpanes in The Newark Museum* (Newark, N.J.: The Newark Museum, 1948), p. 15.

42. *Godey's Lady's Book,* 91 (July–December 1875), p. 510.

43. Earle, *Customs and Fashions,* p. 31.

44. Charles C. Andrews, *History of the New-York African Free-Schools* (New York: Mahlon Day, 1830; reprint ed., New York: Negro Universities Press, 1969), pp. 54, 110.

45. Florence Hartley, *The Ladies' Handbook of Fancy and Ornamental Work* (Philadelphia: J. W. Bradley, 1859), pp. 239–240.

46. Lenice Ingram Bacon, *American Patchwork Quilts* (New York: William Morrow, 1973), pp. 115–116.

47. Catharine Esther Beecher, *A Treatise on Domestic Economy, for the Use of Young Ladies at Home and at School* (New York: Harper & Brothers, 1855), p. 324.

48. Lydia Maria Child, *The Girls' Own Book* (New York: Clark Austin, 1833), p. 225.

49. Lydia Maria Child, *American Frugal Housewife,* 21st ed. (New York: Samuel & William Wood, 1838), pp. 1–2.

50. Beecher and Stowe, *The American Woman's Home,* p. 229.

51. Mary Schenck Woolman, *A Sewing Course* (Washington, D.C.: Frederick A. Fernall, 1911), pp. 31–32.

52. Francis Everett Blake, *History of the Town of Princeton in the County of Worcester and Commonwealth of Massachusetts, 1759–1915,* vol. I, chap. 12: Diary of Elizabeth Fuller (Privately published), p. 309.

53. Blanche Brown Bryant and Gertrude Elaine Baker, eds., *The Diaries of Sally and Pamela Brown, 1832–1838,* 2d ed. (Springfield, Vt.: William L. Bryant Foundation, 1979), pp. 9–10, 11–33, 38–39, 74.

54. Alice Morse Earle, ed., *Diary of Anna Green Winslow* (Williamstown, Mass.: Corner House Publishers, 1974), p. 62.

55. Channing, *Laura Russell Remembers,* pp. 13, 22.

56. M. H. Jewell, ed., *Diary of Sarah Connell Ayer, Portland, Maine* (Portland: Lefavour-Tower Co., 1910), p. 209.

57. Patricia Cooper and Norma Bradley Buferd, *The Quilters: Women and Domestic Art* (New York: Doubleday & Co., 1977), p. 49.

58. Dolores Hinson, *Quilting Manual* (New York: Hearthside Press, 1966), p. 140.

59. Ruth E. Finley, *Old Patchwork Quilts and the Women Who Made Them* (Philadelphia and London: J. B. Lippincott, 1929), pp. 138–140.

60. Charles E. Bentley, *Artamo Colonial Patchwork Quilts, Coverlets, etc.,* Book no. 2 (New York: Bentley-Franklin, 1916).

61. Interview on April 29, 1979, with Mrs. Hazel Kile, eighty-one years old, of Lake View, Iowa, maker of *Alice in Calicoland,* winner of the first prize at the Iowa State Fair, 1976.

62. Beecher and Stowe, *The American Woman's Home*, p. 298.

63. At the Museum of the City of New York.

64. Flora Gill Jacobs, *A History of Dolls' Houses* (New York: Charles Scribner's Sons, 1965), p. 364.

65. Elizabeth Leslie, *The House book, or Manual of Domestic Economy* (Philadelphia: Carey and Hart, 1840), pp. 314–315.

66. *Mountain Mist Blue Book of Quilts* (Cincinnati, Ohio: Stearns & Foster Co., 1937).

BIBLIOGRAPHY

American Museum in Britain. *The American Quilt Tradition: an exhibition to mark the Bi-centenary of American Independence, July 23–September 2, 1976.* Bath: American Museum in Britain, 1976.

Andrews, Charles C. *The History of the New-York African Free-Schools.* New York: Mahlon Day, 1830. Reprint. New York: Negro Universities Press, 1969.

Andrews, Charles M. *Colonial Folkways: A Chronicle of American Life in the Reign of the Georges,* vol. 9. Chronicles of America Series. Edited by Allen Johnson. New Haven, Conn.: Yale University Press, 1919.

Bacon, Lenice Ingram. *American Patchwork Quilts.* New York: William Morrow, 1973.

Bailey, R. B. "Pilgrim Possessions." Manuscript copy, Henry N. Flynt Library of Historic Deerfield, Inc., Deerfield, Massachusetts, 1951.

Beecher, Catharine Esther. *A Treatise on Domestic Economy, for the Use of Young Ladies at Home and at School.* New York: Harper & Brothers, 1855.

———, and Stowe, Harriet Beecher. *The American Woman's Home: or, Principles of Domestic Science.* New York: J.B. Ford, 1869.

Bentley, Charles E. *Artamo Colonial Patchwork Quilts, Coverlets, etc.* Book no. 2. New York: Bentley-Franklin, 1916.

Beyer, Alice. *Quilting.* Chicago: Leisure Hobby Series, 1934.

Bishop, Robert, and Safanda, Elizabeth. *A Gallery of Amish Quilts: Design Diversity from a Plain People.* New York: Dutton Paperbacks, 1976.

———, and Coblentz, Patricia. *New Discoveries in American Quilts.* New York: Dutton Paperbacks, 1975.

Blake, Francis Everett. *History of the Town of Princeton in the County of Worcester and Commonwealth of Massachusetts, 1759–1915,* vol. 1, chap. 12: Diary of Elizabeth Fuller. Privately published.

Bryant, Blanche Brown, and Baker, Gertrude Elaine, eds. *The Diaries of Sally and Pamela Brown, 1832–1838, and Hyde Leslie, 1887, of Plymouth Notch, Vermont.* 2d ed. Springfield, Vt.: William L. Bryant Foundation, 1979.

Carlisle, Lilian Baker. *18th & 19th Century American Art at Shelburne Museum.* Museum Pamphlet Series, no. 5. Shelburne, Vt.: Shelburne Museum, 1960.

Carter, Lydia A. *The Discovery of a Grandmother.* Newtonville, Mass.: Henry H. Carter, 1920.

Channing, Marion L., ed. *Laura Russell Remembers.* Manuscript copy, Pilgrim Hall, Plymouth, Massachusetts. New Bedford, Mass.: Reynolds-DeWalt Printing, 1970.

Child, Lydia Maria. *The American Frugal Housewife, Dedicated to Those Who Are Not Ashamed of Economy.* 21st ed. New York: Samuel & William Wood, 1838.

———. *The Girls' Own Book.* New York: Clark Austin, 1833.

Children's Magazine. October 15, 1912.

Colby, Averil. *Patchwork Quilts.* New York: Charles Scribner's Sons, 1965.

———. *Quilting.* New York: Charles Scribner's Sons, 1971.

Colonial Coverlet Guild of America. *Heirlooms from Old Looms, a Catalogue of Coverlets.* Chicago: R.R. Donnelley & Sons, 1940.

Cooper, Patricia, and Buferd, Norma Bradley. *The Quilters: Women and Domestic Art.* New York: Doubleday & Co., 1977.

Creekmore, Betsey B., and Creekmore, Betsey. *Your World in Miniature: A Guide to Making Small-Scale Rooms and Scenes.* New York: Doubleday & Co., 1976.

Cummings, Abbott Lowell. *Bed Hangings: A Treatise on Fabrics and Styles in the Curtaining of Beds: 1650–1850.* Boston: The Society for the Preservation of New England Antiquities, 1961.

———. *Rural Household Inventories, 1675–1775.* Boston: The Society for the Preservation of New England Antiquities, 1964.

Cunnington, Phyllis, and Buck, Ann. *Children's Costume in England in the 14th through 19th Centuries.* London: Adam & Charles Buck, 1965.

———, and Lucas, Catherine. *Costume for Births, Marriages and Deaths.* New York: Barnes & Noble Books, 1972.

Davidson, Mary Ann Ferrin. "An Autobiography and Reminiscence." *Annals of Iowa,* 3d ser., 37, no. 4 (Spring 1964).

The Denver Art Museum. *Quilts and Coverlets.* Denver, Colo.: The Denver Art Museum, 1974.

"Diary of Eliza Babcock Leonard," Greenfield, Massachusetts, August 19, 1841–June 13, 1850. Manuscript copy in the collection of the Pocumtuck Valley Memorial Association, Deerfield, Massachusetts.

Dunton, William Rush, Jr., M.D. *Old Quilts.* Catonsville, Md.: William Rush Dunton, 1947.

Earle, Alice Morse. *Child Life in Colonial Days.* New York: The Macmillan Company, 1899.

———. *Customs and Fashions in Old New England.* New York: Charles Scribner's Sons, 1893.

———, ed. *Diary of Anna Green Winslow.* Williamstown, Mass.: Corner House Publishers, 1974.

"English Furniture Exports to America, 1697–1830." *Antiques, a Magazine for Collectors and Amateurs* (January 1964).

Finley, Ruth E. *Old Patchwork Quilts and the Women Who Made Them.* Philadelphia and London: J.B. Lippincott, 1929.

Fitzrandolph, Mavis. *Traditional Quilting: Its Story and Its Practice.* London: B.T. Batsford, 1954.

Glaister, Elizabeth. *Needlework.* London: Macmillan & Co., 1880.

Godey's Lady's Book. January 1835, and vol. 91, July–December 1875.

Haders, Phyllis. *Sunshine and Shadow: The Amish and Their*

Quilts. New York: Universe Books/The Main Street Press, 1976.

Hake, Elizabeth. *English Quilting, Old and New, with Notes on Its West Country Tradition.* London: B.T. Batsford, 1937.

Hall, Carrie A., and Kretsinger, Rose G. *The Romance of the Patchwork Quilt in America.* Caldwell, Idaho: Caxton Printers, 1935.

Hall, Eliza Calvert [pseud.]. *Aunt Jane of Kentucky.* Boston: Little, Brown, 1908.

———. *A Book of Hand-Woven Coverlets.* Boston: Little, Brown, 1912.

Hartley, Florence. *The Ladies' Handbook of Fancy and Ornamental Work.* Philadelphia: J.W. Bradley, 1859.

Heisey, John W. *Checklist of American Coverlet Weavers.* Williamsburg, Va.: Colonial Williamsburg Foundation, 1978.

Hinson, Dolores. *Quilting Manual.* New York: Hearthside Press, 1966.

Hobbies (January 1942). Chicago: Lightner Publishing Co., 1942.

Holstein, Jonathan. *Abstract Design in American Quilts.* New York: Whitney Museum of American Art, 1971.

———. *The Pieced Quilt, an American Design Tradition.* Greenwich, Conn.: New York Graphic Society, 1973.

Iverson, Marion Day. "The Bed Rug in Colonial America." *Antiques, a Magazine for Collectors and Amateurs* (January 1964).

Ives, Suzy. *Patterns for Patchwork Quilts and Cushions.* Newton Centre, Mass.: Charles T. Branford, 1977.

Jacobs, Flora Gill. *A History of Dolls' Houses.* New York: Charles Scribner's Sons, 1965.

Jewell, M. H., ed. *Diary of Sarah Connell Ayer, Portland, Maine.* Portland: Lefavour-Tower Co., 1910.

Johnson, Bruce, *et al. A Child's Comfort: Baby and Doll Quilts in American Folk Art.* New York: Harcourt Brace Jovanovich in association with the Museum of American Folk Art, 1977.

"The Journal of Sarah Davenport, May 1, 1849, Through May 16, 1852." *The New Canaan Historical Society Annual* (June 1950).

Katzenberg, Dena S. *The Great American Cover-up: Counterpanes of the 18th & 19th Centuries.* Baltimore: The Baltimore Museum of Art, 1971.

Larcom, Lucy. *A New England Girlhood.* Boston and New York: Houghton Mifflin, 1892.

Leslie, Eliza. *American Girl's Book or Occupation for Play Hours.* 14th ed. Boston: Munroe & Francis, 1849.

———. *The House Book, or Manual of Domestic Economy.* Philadelphia: Carey & Hart, 1840.

Louvre, musée des arts décoratifs. *Quilts* (catalogue). Paris: Palais du Louvre, 1972.

MacKay, James. *Nursery Antiques.* London: Ward Locke, 1976.

McClinton, Katharine Morrison. *Antiques of American Childhood.* New York: Clarkson N. Potter, 1970.

McKim, Ruby Short. *One Hundred and One Patchwork Patterns.* Independence, Mo.: McKim Studios, 1931.

Newman, Thelma R. *Quilting, Patchwork, Appliqué and Trapunto.* New York: Crown Publishers, 1974.

The New-York Historical Society. Estate Inventories of the seventeenth and eighteenth centuries.

150 Years of American Quilts (catalogue). Lawrence: University of Kansas Museum of Art, 1973.

O'Brien, Marian Maeve. *Collector's Guide to Dollhouses and Dollhouse Miniatures.* New York: Hawthorn Books, 1974.

Orlofsky, Patsy, and Orlofsky, Myron. *Quilts in America.* New York: McGraw-Hill Book Co., 1974.

Pearse, Ouida. *Quilting.* London: Sir Isaac Pitman & Sons, 1934.

Peterson, Harold L. *Americans at Home: from the Colonists to the Late Victorians.* New York: Charles Scribner's Sons, 1971.

Peto, Florence. *Historic Quilts.* New York: American Historical Company, 1939.

Pforr, Effie Chalmers. *Progressive Farmer Award Winning Quilts.* Birmingham, Ala.: Oxmoor House, 1974.

Rabb, Kate Milner. *Indiana Coverlets and Coverlet Weavers,* 8, no. 8. Indianapolis: Indiana Historical Society Publications, 1928.

Reinert, Guy F. "Pennsylvania Dutch Coverlets." *Home Craft Course,* 9. Kutztown, Pa.: Mrs. C. Naaman Keyser, 1947.

Robertson, Elizabeth Wells. *American Quilts.* New York: The Studio Publications, 1948.

Safford, Carleton L., and Bishop, Robert. *America's Quilts and Coverlets.* New York: E. P. Dutton, 1972.

Schorsch, Anita. *Images of Childhood.* New York: Mayflower Books, 1979.

Scott, Beatrice. *The Craft of Quilting, with a Note on Patchwork by Anne Heynes.* Leicester, England: The Dryad Press, 1935.

Sheldon Memorial Art Gallery. *Quilts in Nebraska, an Exhibition Presented in Collaboration with the Lincoln Quilters Guild* (catalogue), *September 17–October 13, 1974.* Lincoln: University of Nebraska, 1974.

Stearns and Foster Company. *The Mountain Mist Blue Book of Quilts.* Cincinnati: Lockland, 1937.

Still, George Frederic. *The History of Paediatrics: The Progress of the Study of Diseases of Children up to the End of the XVIIIth Century.* London: Oxford University Press, 1931. Reprint. London: Dawsons of Pall Mall, 1965.

Swygert, Mrs. Luther M., ed. *Heirlooms from Old Looms: A Catalog of Coverlets Owned by The Colonial Coverlet Guild of America and Its Members.* Chicago: Mrs. Harold E. Sanke, 1955.

Victoria and Albert Museum, Department of Textiles. *Notes on Quilting.* London: published under the authority of the Board of Education and Kynoch Press, 1932.

Webster, Marie D. *Quilts: Their Story and How to Make Them.* New York: Doubleday, Page, 1915.

"What Is American Folk Art? A Symposium." *Antiques, a Magazine for Collectors and Amateurs* (May 1950).

White, Margaret E. *Quilts and Counterpanes in The Newark Museum.* Newark, N.J.: The Newark Museum, 1948.

Wishy, Bernard. *The Child and the Republic.* Philadelphia: University of Pennsylvania Press, 1968.

Woolman, Mary Schenck. *A Sewing Course.* Washington, D.C.: Frederick A. Fernall, 1911.

INDEX